HOW TO HANDLE
CLAIMS AND RETURNS

IRWIN R. KISSEL

ANN KISSEL GRUN

HOW TO HANDLE CLAIMS AND RETURNS

A Manual for Manufacturers and Retailers

McGRAW-HILL BOOK COMPANY

New York St. Louis San Francisco London
Düsseldorf Johannesburg Kuala Lumpur
Rio de Janeiro Singapore Toronto
Montreal Mexico Sydney
Panama New Delhi

Library of Congress Cataloging in Publication Data

Kissel, Irwin R
How to handle claims and returns.

1. Customer service. 2. Complaints (Retail trade)
I. Grun, Ann Kissel, joint author. II. Title.
HF5415.5.K54 658.8'12 73-3316
ISBN 0-07-034897-9

1234567890 BPBP 76543

The editors for this book were W. Hodson Mogan and Carolyn Nagy, the designer was Naomi Auerbach, and its production was supervised by Teresa F. Leaden. It was set in Caledo by University Graphics, Inc.
It was printed and bound by The Book Press.

CONTENTS

PREFACE

In an area where no formal, authoritative published text appears, this book blends the results of many years of practical experience with modern research by attempting to bridge the complaints of retailers and manufacturers of soft goods and to bring the parties involved into a more harmonious interrelationship. Both the retailers and the manufacturers in the soft goods industry are being confronted with claims, returns, and penalties in ever-increasing volume.

Retailers complain of the high percentage of returns from consumers, the extra costs involved in these transactions, the poor quality of workmanship, the lack of inspection, partial shipments, improper invoicing, failure to combine and consolidate shipments, and a general deterioration of service by the resources to their customers.

The resources complain of penalty charges for the slightest deviation from confirmations, the higher costs of combining shipments, the extra costs involved in making shipments to branch stores, or individual packing for each branch to be shipped to a central warehouse, for which they receive no extra compensation.

Confirmations from stores are in almost unreadable fine print, with many onerous clauses, and the requirements of each store are different and complex, making computer handling of these impractical and costly.

This manual explains in clear, nontechnical terms the Interstate Commerce Commission and Federal Trade Commission regulations in such matters, and it covers federal laws, transportation rules and regulations, and accepted trade practices. This permits the claims department to be in a position to refute unjustified claims and make the correct decisions in the handling of claims and returns. By judicious handling, satisfactory customer relationships are maintained and open deductions from customers' remittances are kept to a minimum.

The manual also includes twenty-one cross-referenced, "hard-to-write" letters, which have resulted in the successful recovery of claims worth thousands of dollars which were deducted from remittances. Five new forms are suggested. Use of these should prevent recurrence of justified claims, returns, and penalties.

Based on many years of experience in factoring, textile manufacturing, converting, retailing, garment manufacturing, and marketing, the authors have developed proven, successful procedures, which should standardize the handling of claims and returns, and which should be beneficial to all concerned. It should prove of especially great value to the managers of the thousands of stores run by national chains. Most managers are trained in merchandising, inventory control, buying, personnel hiring, and supervision, and should find the knowledge explained and detailed in this manual a considerable asset.

The subject of claims and returns is not being taught in textile or technical schools at this time. With this manual, the student will become aware of the governmental rules and trade practices that he will have to deal with, whether he becomes connected with the retail, manufacturing, or distribution end of the industry.

Many books have been written about fabric and manufacturing defects. This manual discusses the more difficult, most controversial, and least understood types of claims, such as latent defects (obnoxious odors and their removal), skin allergies, flammability lawsuits, migration, and subordination. It instructs the reader how to protect himself when such claims occur or develop, what steps are to be taken, and the insurance coverage required to minimize and avoid such losses. It lays special stress on the subject of transportation, since experience has shown that more claims develop from transportation problems than from any other areas.

The book also shows the proper way to handle claims and returns due to "concealed loss (shortage) and concealed damage" by the consignors of shipments. Carriers' rules regarding notification of loss, inspection, and the time limits that apply are detailed.

Included are rules and regulations concerning ownership and who shall file the claim, legal statutory time limits, tracing shipments, filing a claim, and salvage. The practical and detailed methods of handling claims, returns, and penalties, and the problems that arise are covered, as well as cycle follow-up and notification to all concerned parties.

By the adoption and application of this manual, profits should be increased because of the resulting lower cost in the handling of claims and returns and the recovery of deductions that should have been made against others. It can be used as a training manual for many positions in manufacturing and retailing, and as a reference text for supervisors and managers in retailing, garment manufacturing, fabric manufacturing, and distribution.

The authors advocate the adoption of a uniform purchase order to be agreed to by the respective associations of retailing and manufacturing. This will permit both parties to handle the shipping and receiving of merchandise ordered and to be in such a form that can be properly handled by data processing.

This manual is intended as a practical treatise on the handling of claims and returns which will hopefully become the "code" of the retailing and manufacturing industries.

The authors wish to express their appreciation and thanks to Reginald C. G. Witt, executive director of the National Freight Claim Council, for his assistance in the preparation of the chapters concerning transportation.

Irwin R. Kissel
Ann Kissel Grun

HOW TO HANDLE CLAIMS AND RETURNS

chapter one

HOW TO HANDLE CLAIMS

Handling Systematically

As volume increases, so does the number of claims, and unless the claims are handled in a systematic manner, they will soon engulf you.

Notification of Claims

Claims are presented in many ways:

By debit memo
By letter
By telephone
By a buyer
By a resident buying office
By a salesman
By deduction from a remittance

Claim Clerk

All persons and offices receiving claims should immediately refer them to the claim clerk. By doing so, a central follow-up system is initiated, and all claims, no matter how small, are periodically handled and resolved as quickly as possible, in accordance with company policy.

By referring the claim at once to the claim clerk, one does not become involved in the time-consuming details of handling claims.

Those receiving the claims by telephone should not make note of the details but should transfer the call to the claim clerk. In that person's absence, the caller's name and phone number should be obtained and the call returned by the claim clerk.

The above procedure is followed because it is the job of the claim clerk to ask the necessary questions to expedite the settlement of the claim; the information obtained by others is usually so incomplete as to require the claim clerk to again question the consignee, much to that person's annoyance.

Original Papers

Original papers should always be retained by the claim clerk. If it is necessary to refer to another division of the company or enlist its assistance, only copies of the documents should be sent.

Sales personnel are prone to misfile, mislay, such documents, with the result that the systematic follow-up cycle will fail, and the claim will remain unresolved.

Dating Documents

All claims and documents should be date-stamped. Telephone calls should be recorded: the caller's name should be written and the date stamped.

Remittance slips with the first indication of a claim should be copied and date-stamped upon receipt. The date is important, particularly if the notice of a claim comes at such a late date as to outlaw any recovery from any party responsible for the loss incurred.

Preliminary Examination of Claim

The claim clerk makes a preliminary study of each claim to determine if all the necessary information is available to properly investigate and resolve the claim.

Claim Inquiry Form

If the claim slip requires further information and is incomplete, it may be necessary to send a claim inquiry form in duplicate to the customer for the additional information. A copy of the claim inquiry should be attached to the claim papers and placed in the follow-up cycle folder.

Small Claims

Small shortage claims of up to $15 or three-twelfths of a dozen are usually allowed without further follow-up because they are too costly to research and follow up.

Customer's Claim and Credit Index Card

For each customer there is a credit index card which is also used as a claim card. (See form on page 125.)

The date and amount of shortage claims and unjustified claims are entered, along with the reasons, to determine if a customer is a constant claimer—especially regarding small claims. When there are many small claims, the account is investigated and evaluated as to its profitability.

Supporting Information

When a claim has to be followed up, the following support papers may be necessary:

Copy of claim
Copy of invoice

Copy of receipt (original bill of lading)
Copy of order
Copy of confirmation of order
Copy of advertising agreement

Keeping Claims Separately

Papers for each claim should be kept separate from the papers for other claims, even if the claims are similar in type, since much time and effort will be expended in resolving a particular claim.

Letters to customers and the distribution plant should deal with a single claim, for the reasons given above.

Follow-up Cycle

Claims are kept alphabetically by claimant in a follow-up cycle folder for quick access when needed.

Long-distance calls are often received from customers in response to letters sent to them regarding claims; thus the file should be readily available.

Papers for claims for amounts under $50 are kept in one folder, and when time is pressing, the claims should be reviewed at least every two weeks, although a weekly review is preferable.

Papers for claims for amounts over $50 are kept in a separate folder, and the claims are reviewed with the controller each week.

It is best to set a definite hour for review to ensure a systematic follow-up.

Before a review, the claim clerk updates each claim with responses from the customer and distribution plant, with records of remittances, or with other data concerning the claim.

A systematic follow-up not only serves to quickly and properly resolve a claim; it also serves as a deterrent to the filing of new, and especially small, claims, since customers know that the claims will have the attention of the resource.

Controller

If two letters are sent a week apart and there is no reply, a third letter is sent on a week later, threatening to refer the matter to the controller. (See Letter A on page 49.)

It is embarrassing for the consignee's employees to have the controller intercede, so that the third letter should result in a prompt response.

If there is no reply to the third letter within a week, a letter is sent to the controller enlisting his support. (See Letter B on page 50.)

Telephone Calls

If no response is received from a small store after three letters, or if no reply is received from the controller, then a call to the owner of the small store or to the controller is usually productive in resolving the matter.

Buyer's Assistance

If the matter remains unresolved, the buyer's assistance is requested.

Salesman's Cooperation

After the controller has been contacted, the salesman is apprised of the situation. His assistance is requested, inasmuch as his business with the account may be affected if the matter is not equitably resolved.

Unresolved Claim

If the amount of the claim is small, the advertising budget for that store is reduced.

If the amount is sizable, it is helpful to know the volume of business done with the account on a seasonal and annual basis, in order to determine whether or not to compromise the claim, prosecute the claim, or close the account.

Customer's Index Card in the Distribution Plant

Customer index cards, filed alphabetically by state, are maintained by the distribution plant. (See form on page 126.)

The reason the cards are filed by state is that in the case of a salesman's change, catalog mailing, or other notice, the name plates, also kept alphabetically by state, can easily be corrected, updated, and kept current.

The index card is important in avoiding errors in filling the customer's orders and in following their specifications.

With the advent of stores' penalties, prior notice of a store's rules will prevent errors that may lead to the store imposing penalties.

Each large department store and chain has many regulations peculiar to it.

It is time-consuming to read the fine print of a store's confirmation every time an order is received, but once the major points are recorded on the index card, a review of additional orders will not be necessary.

In its interest to handle orders and shipments in an economical manner, the store should keep its resources informed whenever there is an important change in its confirmation as it affects the filling and transportation of its orders.

Copy of Index Card Attached to Order

When an order is received at the distribution plant, a copy of the index card should be attached to the order. This procedure will alert the picker, packer, shipper, and biller to the store's requirements. (See form on page 126.)

This should be helpful in observing the general terms of the confirmation and avoiding penalty charges.

Penalty Charges

Stores are increasingly assessing penalty charges for the slightest alleged errors of the suppliers and their distribution plants. (See form on page 58.)

These charges, varying from $1 to $25 are the store's assessment of the additional cost to them, and there is no prior agreement as to the amount to be charged.

With the advent of branch stores, central distribution facilities, and the consolidation of shipments, there has been a noticeable increase of claims regarding shortages, packaging, and transportation, as well as invoicing.

In addition to the amount of the penalty charge, the cost of the time required by the resource to investigate the charge may exceed the amount of the charge.

This is especially true for multiple store shipments made "after cancellation date," as the total penalty charges may exceed any profit on the shipment.

Shipments made "after cancellation date" should be cleared with the buyer; if such shipments are approved, the agreement should be noted on the invoice, along with the buyer's name and with the additional remark "no penalty to be charged." If not, customer may refuse shipment.

With the advent of computerization, it is proving exceedingly difficult to observe all the particular requirements of a specific store. The computers are programmed to handle the general requirements of the trade and most of its customers as to invoicing, packaging, and routing.

It would be best for all concerned if the resources, through their associations and the National Retail Merchants Association, could agree on a standard order form so that just penalties of a reasonable amount could be charged for avoidable errors on both parties' part.

The present system of individual stores assessing penalty charges can only lead to extra work for both parties, as well as to confrontation, dissatisfaction, and extra costs.

Customer's Index Card

Whenever a penalty charge is assessed, the claim clerk should advise the distribution plant so that the customer's index card can be marked with the information needed to prevent future penalty charges. (See form on page 126.)

Claimers

Some accounts are known as "claimers." The mere knowledge that their claims will be fully investigated and challenged when incorrect deters the claimers from making as many claims as they normally would.

Unfortunately, many resources issue credit immediately upon receipt of a claim because they lack the personnel to investigate the claim or because they believe it is less costly to allow the claim than to properly investigate it, in the light of the salary and time of the personnel involved in checking claims.

Libel

Care must be taken not to make any libelous accusations against customers, customers' employees, and transportation companies and their employees. The resource's employees must use discretion in their spoken and written communications.

Copies to Salesman

Copies of all correspondence with customers affecting dating, pricing, routing, and advertising are sent to the salesman and sales manager for their future guidance.

Accounts Receivable

Copies need not be sent to accounts receivable, for the claim clerk's desk should be near accounts receivable ledgers, and the claim clerk should have access to these books.

Claim clerks should mark the customer's ledger as to pending claims so that accounts receivable can promptly notify the claim clerk of any deduction or remittance affecting a claim.

Types of Claims

Terms, interest charges, and dating
Pricing
Shortages
Damages
Transportation
Returns
Advertising
Penalty charges

chapter two

TERMS AND DATING

Dating as the First

Some firms, probably most, automatically extend as the "first of the month" invoices on shipments made after the 25th of the month. Other firms extend the dating as the "first of the month" on shipments made after the 20th of the month.

Late Arrival of Shipments

Customers receiving shipments later than usual may request extra dating. Some of the reasons given for late arrival and extra dating are as follows:

Abnormal transportation delay
Improper address
Damage claim . . . awaiting inspection
Shortage claim . . . awaiting inspection
Partial delivery of order

Such requests, if warranted, are usually granted.

New-store Openings

New stores or new branches of existing stores may request extra dating from thirty to ninety days.

Extra dating is usually arranged for a maximum of sixty days.

Continental U.S.A.

Stores in the areas of Hawaii, Alaska, Guam, etc., are given on request an extra thirty days to compensate for the extended arrival time. This extra dating permits the stores to check the shipments before payment is required.

Prearranged Dating

A number of customers whose large volume with the resource warrants special considerations require extra dating from thirty to sixty days on all purchases. Their volume is too great for their working capital, and with the approval of the credit department the extra dating is usually granted.

Promotions

To encourage early purchasing and shipment, some groups of styles or lines are offered with extra dating, which could amount to sixty to ninety days. For example, fall styles, ordinarily shipped about August 25, are offered for sale and shipment as early as May 25, with dating as of August 25. Such promotions may be offered with price concessions as well.

Group Purchases

Buying offices arranging group purchases similarly arrange extra dating, or earlier shipment with dating.

Some orders received directly from individual stores not recognized as being members of the group are not given the extra dating, but extra dating is granted upon request.

Credit Approval

The credit department has the right to limit or deny extra dating despite the promotional offering if the account's credit does not permit the extra dating or if the customer's previous payment record is poor, thus making extra dating unwarranted.

Unjustified Extra Dating

Some customers, usually those whose credit is questionable, habitually request extra dating on every invoice—in many instances without offering any explanation or reason.

Such requests are usually declined.

Confirmation of Orders

Confirmations of orders may be received, marked with requests for extra dating. This change from a previous arrangement may go unnoticed by clerks, and such requests may have to be granted.

In Advance of Shipping Date

The distribution plant may, through error or for compelling reasons, make shipments in advance of the customer's shipping date. When this is called to the attention of the resource, extra dating is granted.

chapter three

INTEREST CHARGES

Delaying Payments

Charges for interest on late payments and for repayment of unjustified deductions are difficult to collect, especially when interest rates are high.

Even the most prestigious name stores resort to questionable tactics to avoid and delay payment:

Improper dating of checks and mailing at a later date
Skipping invoices
Requesting proof of delivery
Making unjustified deductions for claims they should have made against the carrier

Collecting Interest Charges

The best way to collect interest charges is to bill the store for the interest instead of sending a letter or statement.

Be sure to list the invoices against which the interest charges apply, as well as the department number and order number.

In this way there will be no excuse for the store to avoid repayment by stating that it cannot properly apply the invoice.

If the store persists in not paying incurred interest charges, the advertising budget allotted to the store should be reduced accordingly.

Resources with well-known brand-name products that are in demand can maintain a firm stance in this regard.

chapter four

PRICES

Regular Prices

Regular prices are listed on weekly delivery charts and conform to samples, price lists, and catalog.

Reduced Prices

Reduced prices, when authorized, may be telephoned to key salesmen and are noted on weekly delivery charts.

The dates of such marked-down prices should be recorded. Some customers, when making payments for styles purchased before the markdown date, pay for the styles at the reduced price.

Letters quoting the markdown date and voiding the deductions are sent to the customers. (See Letter A on page 50.)

Net Prices

Most chains, exporters, and some customers purchase on a net basis.

Charts showing the net prices of the gross prices usually quoted should be provided to the sales staff so that the properly figured net prices appear on the order.

Some buyers using their own system of figuring net prices invariably favor themselves by a few cents per item or dozen.

Incorrect Prices

Salesmen, in forwarding their orders, will often list an incorrect price if they use the memory system instead of looking at the delivery chart price, catalog, or tag on the garment.

Clerks, checking the orders, are supposed to catch such errors.

Price-Change Card

When the price is incorrect, or when the delivery listed is incorrect, a card listing order number and department number covering the situation should be sent to the customer. The order should be marked "P.C." (price change) to facilitate dealing with any deduction or payment at the incorrect price. (See form on page 124.)

Confirmation of Order

The confirmation of order may accompany the original order sent in by the salesman, or it may be received separately at a later date.

These confirmations may list a price incorrectly and should be checked against the price list and original unconfirmed order.

A price-change notice should be sent.

Refunds in the case of an uncorrected price are often difficult to collect, as the store may maintain that its markup was based on the price of its order.

Sending a copy of the price list prevailing at the approximate date of the order may prove successful in convincing the store that the price on its confirmation is incorrect.

Group Purchases

Buyers for a group may arrange a lower price for styles or a special collection of styles. Often a store in that group will send in an order directly to the resource, and the clerk may not recognize that the store is a member of that group and charge the regular price.

A debit memo for the price difference invariably follows and must be honored.

Regular Price after Promotion

A promotion planned to encourage earlier purchase and delivery has a termination date. After the termination date, the reduced price reverts to the regular, higher price. Orders may be received after the termination date. A discussion must be held with the sales manager to reach an agreement as to whether or not the orders at the reduced price should be accepted.

If an order is not acceptable, the store must be notified and must agree to a revision of the price before the order can be processed.

Failure to observe the above procedure will make any deduction impossible to recover.

Reorders at the Promotional Price

Reorders at the promotional price present the same problems as described above, and the same procedure follows.

Markdown Money

A customer may have purchased styles for an advertisement or catalog, or he may have purchased too large a quantity of a style or group of styles, only to find that the anticipated sales did not materialize.

While goods are not sold on memorandum or the sales guaranteed, great pressure is brought by the buyer (usually inspired by the merchandise manager) to return all or part of the unsold goods.

Depending on the lateness of the season, the value of the account, and the pressure of the resident buying office, the sales manager may authorize all or part of the return, or he may try to induce the buyer to accept markdown money.

This alternative may be preferable, especially if the return would be so late that the resource would have to markdown the goods anyway and then endeavor to resell them or be forced to carry them over to the next season, thus incurring costly interest carrying charges.

If the buyer accepts the markdown money, a price allowance notice must be sent to the claim clerk so that credit may be issued (and the commission on the sale changed accordingly).

Change in Buyers

Buyer changes always present problems to the resource. New buyers may find styles they do not care for, or which were purchased in quantity and did not sell. The buyers then try to clean house—too often at the resource's expense.

The same conditions prevail as described in the section on markdown money, and the solutions may be the same.

Overpricing

A number of the larger stores which do extensive advertising have resorted to an overpricing arrangement in order to obtain a greater grant of advertising money from their resources than they are entitled to have.

They will build up the prices on a number of styles and use the overage as an advertising allowance.

For example, if style number 1000 regularly sells for $45 a dozen, the store will request that it be billed at $51 a dozen, thus accumulating $6 a dozen for advertising expenses.

Care must be taken that the discount, usually 8 percent, be deducted so that the net advertising allowance per dozen is only $5.52. This is important, as all advertising deductions are on a net basis.

All orders with overpricing must be accompanied by an overpricing form on which full information and extensions are listed. Consequently, when the debit memo is received it can easily be checked against the overpricing form.

Large mail-order chains are resorting to overpricing. In such cases, because the number of invoices affected can be great, all orders (except the customers' copies) should be marked "overpricing," and an extra copy of the invoice so marked should be sent to the claim clerk.

Credit allowances are issued only for overpricing of actual net shipments, since often only part of the style may be shipped because of cancellations, lack of stock, returns, etc.

In a number of instances the advertisement may not run, and the customer may or may not request a refund of the overpricing. A request for a refund is honored.

Underpricing

Underpricing is mostly used by chains and is the reverse of overpricing.

This method enables the customer to sell a style or group of styles at a higher markup percentage than would be allowable if the styles were purchased at a resource's regular price.

The dollar amount accumulated in underpricing is compared with the amount accumulated in overpricing, and the difference is the amount to be accounted for by the resource to the customer.

The detailed recordkeeping is the same as described for overpricing. Underpricing is always accompanied by an overpricing arrangement.

Chains do not send in debit memorandums or advertisements as do department stores when underpricing and overpricing are concerned.

At the end of each month a statement is sent by the resource for the invoices affected during the month. A remittance accompanies the statement if an amount is due to the customer, and a remittance is sent by the customer if an amount is due to the resource.

Department stores using underpricing average the amount directly in their orders, underpaying on certain styles and overpaying on others, so that the dollar differences are equal. Therefore no record or claim is involved.

Issuing Price-claim Credits

A credit authorization due to price claims must be marked on the show-room copy of the customer's invoice. This prevents the issuance of a duplicate credit or claim against the same invoice. The invoice is marked with the debit number and date and is then returned to the show room for its files.

The distribution plant also marks its invoice copy so that any returns on the particular invoice are credited to the customer at the reduced price.

Salesman's Commissions

All authorizations for price-claim credits must list the invoice number and date so that the commissions paid to the salesman can be adjusted when the price is lowered.

This applies when the salesman's commission agreement calls for a lower commission rate when goods are sold below regular prices.

chapter five

SHORTAGES

Resource Count and Weight

A claim for shortage is difficult to handle because according to the general procedure—at least in theory—shipments leave the distribution plant with the correct number of goods as invoiced.

The picker, checker, and packer have each counted the goods and agreed on the total before the goods have been packed, sealed, and weighed.

Carton Weight

Each carton is weighed, and the weight of each carton is listed on the invoice and bill of lading.

Shipment with Combined Invoices

In this type of shipment one bill of lading includes the cartons of more than one invoice.

All the invoice numbers are listed on the bill of lading and are cross-referenced on the invoices affected.

Consolidated Shipment

In this type of shipment, one bill of lading includes the cartons for branch stores which are shipped to one distribution point.

Because more claims for this type of shipment are received than other claims, and because they are most difficult to handle, the distribution plant double-checks shipments of this type and records the names of the checkers. It places on the packing slip and invoice the following stamp:

> THIS INVOICE COVERS A CONSOLIDATED SHIPMENT THAT HAS BEEN CHECKED AND RECHECKED FOR QUANTITY. WEIGHTS HAVE BEEN VERIFIED. NO CLAIMS FOR SHORTAGES WILL BE ALLOWED.

This clause often deters receiving clerks from filing shortage claims, or it will cause them to wait a reasonable period of time for straggling containers before filing any claim for shortage.

Separate weights for each store's cartons are listed on the bill of lading so that claims can be checked for the individual store and comparisons made of the weights for similar quantities shipped to other branches.

Damaged or Open Cartons

When a customer receives a carton that outwardly appears to be damaged or partly open, an immediate inspection and count should be conducted by the deliverer and consignee and the results noted on the driver's and consignee's receipts.

Merely marking "carton open" or "carton damaged" does not fully establish the quantity missing or damaged.

Recoopered Cartons

A carrier is required to mark the consignee's receipt "recoopered" if, for any reason, he has found it necessary to repack the shipment.

The consignee, so alerted, should demand an immediate count and inspection before signing the receipt to determine if any shortage or damage exists. If any shortage or damage is found, the carriers' and consignee's receipts should be so marked.

Delayed Receipt of Missing Carton

Some consignees, as soon as a shipment is received and a carton or more are found missing, immediately make out a debit memorandum, charging the resource for the alleged shortage.

This procedure is improper, since the claim should be made against the carrier.

Usually straggling or delayed cartons are received the following day, or within a few days. Unfortunately the receiving clerk does not always cancel the debit memorandum or issue a credit memorandum to balance out the shortage claim. This results in a great deal of unnecessary work on the part of the resource in tracing the missing cartons and obtaining a cancellation of the debit memo.

Once a debit memorandum is made out, the store makes a deduction from a remittance.

Perhaps the following incident with a large department store in Philadelphia best describes the situation.

After numerous large claims for shortages, and after the claim clerk had sent numerous letters without receiving any response or repayment, my services were enlisted, and I arranged to visit the store and discuss the matter with the accounts payable manager.

I requested the completed order and the receiving file of the invoices and deductions in question. It soon became evident that the store received the missing cartons a day or two later.

As debit memorandums had already been made out and deductions made from remittances, I asked to see the credit memorandums canceling the charges to the resource.

The accounts payable manager admitted that none had been made out because it was the store's policy not to do so until the resource's efforts made it necessary to do so. He stated that he was opposed to the policy, but he had to abide by it.

He also stated that most resources sent a few letters and finally credited the account and that I was only one of two persons who pursued the matter to a final cancellation of the debit memo—and this was a prestigious store.

Proof of Delivery

When it is determined that a carton or more are missing, proof of delivery is requested. This is best handled through the distribution center, which is closer to the originating carrier and which can obtain such additional information as name of connecting carrier and trailer number.

When there is an urgent need for the missing goods, telephone communication with the original and connecting carriers and with the consignee can be helpful in quickly tracing the missing containers.

One should have the following information available for a quick tracer:

Date of shipment
Routing
Number of cartons
Weight
Pro number
Trailer number

The carrier associations publish lists of their membership, which include their addresses, and the names and telephone numbers of their general managers. These associations cover most of the carriers operating in the United States.

By quickly supplying the consignee with the above information, as well as the date that the shipment was turned over to the connecting carrier and the carrier's name, the resource puts the consignee in a position to more quickly locate the missing shipment, since he is nearer to the point of transfer.

If the cartons cannot be located, the consignee should be notified to file a claim for them under the provisions of "ownership" as explained in the chapter "Returns Due to Transportation Problems."

Entire Shipment Missing

The same procedure applies when an entire shipment is missing as when part of a shipment is missing. The consignee should be notified to file a claim for them under the provisions of "ownership" as explained in the chapter "Returns Due to Transportation Problems."

Conspiracy Shortages

The following experiences with two major department stores in Brooklyn, New York, and Houston, Texas, can best describe large shortage claims:

We had received numerous claims of sizable amounts for concealed shortage. Proof of delivery indicated the receipt of the cartons invoiced, all at one time, so that a straggling carton was not involved.

Numerous letters to the customer went unanswered, and recovery was nowhere in sight.

When the next order was received, the distribution manager was instructed to personally count and verify the quantities being invoiced, and the shipment was made.

As expected, a debit memo was received, again claiming a large concealed shortage. The controller was personally and quietly contacted, and a private surveillance of the area was conducted. (See letter on page 51.)

The receiving clerk and a truckman were apprehended.

The store lost nothing, as a debit memo for the amount stolen was made out and deducted from the resource's invoice. Only the resource was the loser.

The correspondence had been intercepted, and the store was not aware of what had been going on until its attention was called by the resource because of the concealed shortage claims.

The store refunded the full amount previously deducted from the resource, and this type of shortage claims ceased.

In another instance, concerning one of the largest department stores in Los Angeles, hardly a shipment was made without a claim for shortage, though the claims were of small amounts.

Again the controller was contacted, after many letters produced no results. The store claimed (in a form letter) that the receiving clerk personally verified the shortage. (See letter on Shortages, page 52.)

The controller, through a private investigation, determined that there were too many claims to many resources for small shortages. He discovered that a receiving clerk could not accurately count and check off the shipments.

Recovery was made for over ten small shortage claims.

Letters to Consignees

Whenever possible, letters should always be addressed to an individual or to a department, not to the store in general. The customer's debit memo, credit file letters, or previous claims will denote the name of the party to whom the letters should be addressed.

If no name is obtainable, letters should be sent to the traffic department, with copies to accounts payable and the receiving department.

When the name of the proper person or department becomes known, it should be noted on the credit and claim card for future reference.

Letters sent to a store, especially a large store, and not addressed to a particular person or department make the rounds and invariably never reach the proper person.

If a letter or copy of a letter is sent to a buyer, the department number should be added. If a letter is sent to the controller, it should be addressed to him by name.

All such names, in the case of major stores, should be entered on the credit and claim card for future reference.

chapter six

TRANSPORTATION

Shipping Instructions

Many large stores and chains furnish shipping instructions for various weight classifications. However, some of these instructions apply to shipments from the New York area instead of from the distribution plant point of shipment.

If time permits, and for future reference, correct routing instructions should be requested for the point of shipment address.

Claims and penalty charges for not following routing instructions should be rejected.

Routing Instructions

If a customer furnishes a complete routing, listing connecting carriers, the complete routing should appear on the bills of lading and invoices.

The original carrier is not required to use the connecting carrier requested by the customer as long as the connecting carrier's rate is the lowest rate.

Any penalty charges made by the consignee because the originating carrier fails to use the specified connecting carrier should be disallowed and should be charged back to the customer.

If the customer designates only the originating carrier and fails to list a connecting carrier, and charges a penalty for such failure, such penalty should be rejected.

A carrier's duty is to transport the goods with reasonable promptness. This is just as true of connecting carriers as it is of originating carriers.

Best Way

Too many orders, especially from small stores, read "best way."

The people at the distribution plant use their best judgment and select what in their opinion is the best way.

Any claim from customers stating that another carrier would have been faster should be rejected.

Consignees should know the best way from various areas to their particular location, and it should be their responsibility to mark the orders accordingly.

Claims and penalties regarding "best way" should be rejected.

Cheapest Way

The same principles apply to orders marked "cheapest way."

The distribution plant people use their best judgment, but they cannot be expected to know the cheapest way to each location in the United States, especially to the smaller cities.

The stores should know the cheapest way from various areas to their city and should avoid using the designation "cheapest way."

Claims and penalties regarding "cheapest way" should be rejected.

Prepaid Shipments

This should not be confused with FOB store. Prepaid shipments merely concern freight allowances.

Ownership of the goods when placed in the hands of a common carrier is important, as explained in the chapter "Concealed Loss and Damage."

Regarding prepaid shipments, if the prepayment is merely a freight allowance the orders and invoices should be marked:

Freight prepaid, but shipped FOB point of *shipment*

Stores often charge back inward freight charges already paid for by the shipper.

A copy of the bill of lading and paid prepaid freight bill should be attached to a rebilled invoice. Any penalty charges should be rejected.

The same procedure applies to returns made against previously prepaid shipments. Stores charge for inward transportation even though they did not pay the inward transportation cost.

Through Rates

Under ICC regulations, if a "through rate" is specified on the bill of lading and signed for by the originating carrier, such specification is just as binding on the connecting carrier.

Such through rates are thus protected; therefore, any charges other than through rates should not be allowed, and any penalties should be rejected. The consignee should make a claim against the carrier, not against the shipper.

Combined Shipment

Some customers receiving on the same date two or more shipments applying to different orders (especially if one or both shipments are under minimum weights) charge back any excess charges and even impose penalty charges for failure to combine the shipments under one bill of lading. (See Letter A on page 52.)

These charges should be rejected and billed back to the consignee.

Shipments may leave on the same day, although at different times during the day, since trailers leave when packed.

There is usually no agreement to combine shipments of different orders, and in most instances the situation of multiple shipments is impossible to control.

Combined Shipments for Different Divisions

Some customers receiving on the same date two or more shipments applying to different divisions charge back the difference between below-weight minimum freight charges and combined-weight charges. (See Letter B on page 53.)

In addition to the reasons explained in the preceding section, each division may have its own packing and shipping departments. As there is no promise to combine shipments of various divisions, such charges and penalties should be rejected.

Invoices and Packing Slips

Some stores require packing slips and invoices for each carton of every shipment.

If the distribution plant's system is to issue one invoice and one packing slip for each shipment, the customer should be advised when the order is received that the resource cannot comply with the store's requirement.

It is understandable that a distribution plant cannot set up different packing and billing systems for each customer and still operate economically.

Once the customer is notified of the distribution plant's system, any penalty charges for failure to place a packing slip or invoice on the outside of each carton of a shipment should be rejected and rebilled to the customer.

The distribution plant, however, should cross-reference each carton by designating which carton has the packing slip if it is not placed on the outside of the container.

Back Orders

In certain trades, it is customary for the resources to make a partial shipment of orders without being compelled to prepay the charges on back orders. This is especially true when the value of the goods is high and when the cost of transportation does not materially affect the markup.

If the resources make many partial shipments, they can expect charges for the difference in transportation costs and possible penalty charges which they may have to honor.

If a customer specifies no more than two shipments or no more than three shipments, such instructions should be followed unless the resource is willing to ship either prepaid or with an allowance for the difference between the weights.

The distribution plant's index card should be marked whenever a customer charges for "back-order shipments," and the reason for the charge should be noted. The card should also be marked when orders for goods are canceled or goods returned because of back-order shipments.

chapter seven

CONCEALED LOSS AND DAMAGE CLAIM

Theory

At least 90 percent of the consignees of shipments in the soft goods business (and this may be true of all receivers of shipments by common carriers) are unaware or do not have a working knowledge of the regulations instituted by individual truckmen, trucking associations, forwarding associations, and rail associations as well as the Interstate Commerce Commission in their effort to voluntarily resolve claims without the necessity of the claimant taking legal action.

These types of claims are difficult to substantiate because the fault may lie with the shipper, the originating carrier, the connecting carrier, or the consignee.

Any one of the parties connected with the shipment could have caused the concealed loss or damage, and the reason a prompt check of the shipment is made by the consignee is to reduce the time period that the consignee has to account for while the goods were in his possession.

It is therefore important that the consignees and shippers cooperate by carefully following and complying with the regulations established by the carriers governing a prompt inspection whenever a concealed loss or damage occurs.

It is also in the best interests of the consignees and carriers to minimize the loss or damage and to reduce the amount of the claim involved by repairs or other methods or steps that can be taken when such loss or damage occurs.

Definition

A concealed loss or damage is one that could not have been known to exist by an examination of the outside of the containers at the time of delivery.

ICC Regulations

ICC regulations require the carrier to make an inspection, when requested, within a reasonable period and to pay only for those claims for which the carrier is responsible. This rule, if violated, could result in favoring large shippers by reducing the freight rate through payment of unjustified claims for concealed loss or damage.

Carrier's Requirements

ICC regulations do not require a carrier to make a voluntary settlement of any particular claim, but the carriers normally endeavor to do so if they are satisfied that the shipper or the consignee did not contribute to the concealed loss or damage claim.

The claimant is required in the case of a concealed loss or damage claim to establish that neither the shipper nor the consignee could have been responsible for the loss or damage; the claimant does so by certification.

Certification by Shipper

These are standard forms issued by the carriers, available to the shippers, which not only describe the goods, origin, shipper, consignee, way bill or pro number, and loss or damage but require answers to questions regarding packing, picking an order, prior examination, rehandling, protection from theft, and methods of packing.

This must be certified to be true and complete and forwarded to the carrier against whom the claim has been filed.

Certification by Consignee

These are standard forms issued by the carriers, available to the consignees, which not only describe the goods, origin, destination, date of receipt, shipper, and number of contents but require answers to questions regarding details of receipt, hours, date, names of trucking company and drivers, dates of discovery of loss or damage, kind and condition of containers, packing, and space.

This must be certified to be true and complete and forwarded to the carrier against whom the claim has been filed.

Prompt Determination of Loss or Damage

Consignee should check shipments promptly upon arrival. Prompt opening and checking of shipments, reporting of concealed loss or damage as soon as it is discovered, and prompt inspection by the carrier are the best methods of proving that the damage or loss did not occur after the goods were received by the consignee.

When concealed loss or damage is promptly reported to the carrier, the time period during which the consignee possessed the goods is narrowed to the point where there is valid proof that the loss or damage did not occur while the goods were in the consignee's possession.

Movement of Goods after Receipt

Once a concealed loss or damage is discovered and an inspection requested, the consignee should not move the goods or cartons from one area to another. This eliminates the possibility of the carrier claiming that the loss or damage could have resulted after the original delivery was moved to another location.

Carefully preserve any physical indications that the package(s) might have been opened before delivery, such as a difference in sealing tape and inner containers damaged.

Claims for concealed loss or damage will not be paid in full by the carrier unless the evidence shows that the loss or damage could not have occurred after the freight was delivered to the consignee or before it was delivered to the carrier by the shipper.

Where conclusive evidence of responsibility for the concealed loss or damage is not available to the carrier, the carrier may elect to pay all of the claim, refuse any voluntary payment, or offer a compromise settlement of partial payment.

Holding Contents and Containers

The consignee is required to hold the merchandise and containers intact until joint inspection of the containers and material by the carrier and the consignee.

Time Period to Demand Inspection

In the case of a concealed loss or damage claim, the consignee is required, immediately upon discovery of the loss or damage, to demand an inspection by the delivering carrier. The inspection should be requested by phone and immediately confirmed by registered letter, return receipt requested.

Most carriers require that an inspection be requested within fifteen days after receipt of the merchandise. (See letter on page 54.)

If more than fifteen days pass between the date of delivery

of the shipment and the report of loss or damage, it will then be necessary for the claimant to offer reasonable evidence to the carrier's inspector that loss or damage was not incurred by the consignee after delivery of the shipment by the carrier. Any undue delay may violate the rule that the shipping container and its contents be held and be in the same condition they were in where damage was discovered, insofar as it is possible to do so.

Therefore a claim and a request for inspection should be made as soon as possible after the receipt of the goods. However, a number of carriers limit the period within which to demand an inspection to forty-eight hours after receipt of the goods by the consignee.

Determination of Hours for Inspection

Since the carriers under ICC regulations are required to make an inspection within a reasonable time, they can limit the period within which an inspection can be requested. Some carriers shorten the time period for demanding inspection and making an inspection.

It is best for the consignee to obtain from all possible carriers serving its area a copy of the Standard Form for Presentation of Loss or Damage Claim and of the form Inspection Report of Loss or Damage Discovered after Delivery.

The filing of a request for an inspection or the inspection report form by itself does not constitute the legal filing of a claim (see the chapter "Filing of a Claim").

The Standard Form for Presentation of Loss or Damage Claim informs the consignee of the time limit that each carrier requires for both notification of a claim and the period for inspection.

Period for Carrier to Inspect

Most carriers in their inspection report form and their associations state that they are required to make a joint inspection with the consignee within five normal working days (excluding Saturday, Sunday, and holidays) after the receipt of a request for such inspection.

Other carriers do not specify the period within which they will make the joint inspection.

The governmental regulation requires them to make the inspection within a reasonable period. Inasmuch as the consignee is required to hold the merchandise and containers intact pending the inspection, the period cannot be unduly prolonged.

Failure to Inspect within a Reasonable Period

If the carrier fails to make the inspection during the designated time or within a reasonable period, then the consignee should fill out an inspection report and mail same by certified letter, return receipt requested, to the carrier previously requested to make the inspection.

An inspection report made out solely by the consignee will not unreasonably affect any recovery based on the fact that such inspection was made solely by him.

Inspection Report of Concealed Loss or Damage

The Inspection Report of Loss or Damage Discovered after Delivery is an important document. Not only is it informative in the requirements necessary to prove to the carrier that the claimant in no way contributed to the loss or damage but it is a valuable tool in the prosecution of an appeal should the claim be denied or an offered partial settlement be unsatisfactory to the claimant.

Under a proposed rule to be submitted by the ICC for congressional approval, appeals will be arbitrated by them and can be appealed by briefs. Thus a copy of the inspection report will be necessary for such an appeal.

The inspection form also covers salvage, if this is necessary, and its disposition.

A copy of the inspection report should be retained by the claimant.

Release of Merchandise

On claims for losses due to shortage, after an inspection report has been made out and signed by both the carrier's inspector and the consignee, the contents and containers may be released unless the remaining contents are unsalable because of the missing goods.

In such instances, and also when visible open damage to a shipment has been made a matter of record by an inspection report, it shall be the duty of the consignee to retain the damaged merchandise and the shipping container until the carrier desires to take possession of the merchandise as salvage. If the record reflects undisputed carrier liability, the carrier shall take possession of the damaged merchandise as soon as possible, and, in any event, within thirty days from the date the shipment was noted as damaged on the carrier freight bill or from the date of the inspection report if the damage was concealed.

If the carrier does not take possession of the damaged merchandise within the time prescribed above, the consignee shall contact the delivering carrier and request the removal of goods from their premises within fifteen days from the date of their communication. This applies only when the carrier and the consignee agree that the carrier shall handle the disposition of the salvage, and it does not in any manner affect the legal duty that the consignee, when there is substantial value in the salvage, shall accept and handle it in such manner as to mitigate the carrier's loss as much as possible. If there is doubt of carrier liability, the carrier shall so advise the consignee, in which case the consignee may hold the merchandise until the liability of the carrier is determined or may dispose of it so as to mitigate the damage, and the consignee must file claim for such damage.

Carriers shall be required to remove the damaged goods

within the fifteen-day period or advise the consignee that the carrier liability is in doubt and that the damaged merchandise shall be retained by the consignee until the carrier has completed investigation of the claim.

Failure of Consignee to Demand a Timely Inspection

Failure of the consignee to demand a timely inspection or to hold the merchandise and containers intact bars any voluntary settlement by the carrier.

Failure of the consignee to file a demand for inspection within the specified period required by the carrier does not prevent the consignee from filing a legal claim within the statutory limit of nine months, as explained in the section on time limit in the chapter "Filing of a Claim."

Claim by Owner

Claims for concealed loss or damage should be made by the owner.

Ownership is explained in the chapter "Returns Due to Transportation Problems."

Support of Shipper

The shipper should cooperate with the consignee by supplying affidavits, original invoices and bills of lading, certified affidavits, or other documents required by the consignee to support his claim.

If any of these original documents cannot be supplied, a certified copy should be submitted together with a suitable indemnity agreement. (Copies are acceptable only when the originals have been lost or destroyed.)

The indemnity agreement holds the carriers harmless and indemnified against all lawful claims which may be made against them by reason of payment of the original claim.

Failures of Consignee

Most stores, instead of making a claim against the carrier and demanding a timely inspection, forward a debit memorandum directly to the resource, thus making a claim against the wrong party—which is not only improper but is also a violation of the carrier's regulations for the voluntary settlement of claims. (See letter on page 56.)

By so doing, the stores invariably permit the time limitation for demanding an inspection report to expire, and so their claim can then be barred not only by the resource but also by the carrier.

Stores that first advise the resource of a claim by making a deduction and attaching their debit memorandums covering the claim to their remittances will find themselves in a similar position.

Some stores will not conform to the rule of keeping the materials and containers intact and will distribute the merchandise before a timely inspection has been made, thus causing their claims to be denied by the carrier and, subsequently, by the resource. Therefore, it is to the best interests of the consignee to correct the above failures which cause the carrriers to bar concealed loss and damage claims.

Parcel Post

Concealed loss and damage claims can be made for insured parcel-post shipments. The postal manual gives instructions concerning the retention of damaged articles.

It is necessary to retain the containers of goods for which concealed loss and damage claims are bing made.

Consignees must always request inspection for any concealed loss or damage; if the shipper, however, elects to reimburse the consignee for any loss or damage sustained, then the consignee's right to recover should, upon request, be subrogated to the shipper, who may then file a claim against the carrier.

Small Dollar Amount Concealed Loss or Damage

If the consignee's claim for concealed loss or damage is nominal on a fairly large shipment, it would appear to be unreasonable to ask the consignee to hold the contents and all containers for an inspection; only those containers in which concealed loss or damage is present need be retained.

Some carriers may waive inspection for loss or damage claims which are small or inconsequential in nature.

Carriers must be requested to inspect all concealed losses and damages; the carrier had a legal right to waive his right to verify the loss or damage if it is inconsequential, but this is optional with the carrier only, and he is not required to do so.

If the carrier insists on an inspection when the amount is inconsequential, the shipper may elect to issue a credit; the claim card must be so marked to prevent continuous claims of that nature.

Review

Most concealed loss claims are not really loss claims; in most instances, cartons prove to be missing or straggling, and tracers usually account for the missing merchandise when the cartons are delivered at a later date.

Inspections regarding concealed loss claims, other than those involving entire cartons missing, must show that there was empty space in the cartons, when repacked by the inspector, and this is rarely the case.

Receiving clerks, especially on consolidated branch store shipments, are prone to make out a debit memorandum for a shortage, instead of rechecking to see if the error was on the part of their own organization, with one branch receiving goods belonging to another branch.

Claims for damages are different. Damages are apparent and hardly refutable. However, in such cases the consignee frequently does not follow the proper procedure for making the carrier accountable for the loss; instead, the consignee takes the easier course of charging the shipper or returning the damaged goods to the resource without the shipper's consent.

When there is greater cooperation between the consignee and the shipper, neither has to accept an unnecessary loss which rightfully belongs to the carrier. Likewise, a carrier is not required to pay for loss or damage caused by an act or omission of the shipper or consignee. (See letter on page 120.)

chapter eight

ADVERTISING

Theory

Most manufacturers in the soft good field who do a sizable volume of business with the department and specialty stores have an advertising program in one form or another.

This chapter concerns itself only with the granting of advertising allowances by the manufacturers to their customers and the claims and deductions that result.

Purpose of Plan

The purpose of the advertising grant is to increase the volume of sales and to publicize either the manufacturer's name or the trade name, as well as the yarn company's fiber identification when the yarn company contributes toward the dollar cost of the advertising.

Written Agreement

Because of unsatisfactory experience with verbal understandings, most firms have adopted a written form which they require either the buyer or the advertising manager to sign when an advertising grant is made.

This form usually includes the following:

An agreement to pay one-half of the cost up to $ ______
The resource's trade name to appear in the ad
The fiber identification name to appear in the ad
A provision that the tear sheet accompany the bill for the ad

Logos of the company's trade name and fiber identification, if supplied to the stores, are helpful in the proper use of such names.

Types and Places of Advertising

Trade papers
Newspapers
Magazines
Newspaper supplements
Inserts
Mailers
Catalogs
Counter cards and displays
Television
Radio
Modeling
New-store openings
Gifts

Ad Budget Register

Copies of all written agreements are sent to the claim clerk for entry under successive advertising allowance numbers for each division so that the cumulative amount will not exceed the budgeted amount for each division.

Deductions

Problems in claims and deductions arise when the stores violate the written agreement or make an unauthorized deduction for advertising.

Debit Memos and Ads

All debit memos and ads should be approved by the sales manager. The debit memos and ads, together with a copy of the grant, should be sent to the claim clerk for entry in the advertising register so that credit may be given.

The customer's debit memo number should be entered in the register for reference in case the customer takes an unauthorized deduction at a later date.

Recovery from Yarn Companies

The claim clerk, after entering the debit memo and issuing credit, sends to the yarn company a copy of the debit memo and the ad for reimbursement of the amount previously granted to the manufacturer.

No Supporting Ad

If debit memos or deductions from remittances are received without the required accompanying ad, a copy of the ad will be requested before credit is issued.

Unauthorized Ads

Ads and debit memos may be sent by the stores without there being any previous agreement of making a grant to the store.

This may happen because the show room fails to record such an arrangement.

Upon inquiry, the store may advise that the salesman for the account agreed to the grant and failed to notify the sales manager and obtain his consent.

Customers may simply take a grant without authorization.

The sales manager must consider company policy and the advertising budget before determining whether or not to allow a grant.

If a grant is allowed, the usual advertising form is issued. If a grant is disallowed, it is best to have the claim clerk write the letters.

Excess Deductions

Customers may deduct the entire cost of the ad instead of one-half the cost as agreed.

Stores may take an amount in excess of the agreed amount. Again, the sales manager must decide whether to allow the deduction or have the claim clerk endeavor to collect the difference.

Failure to Include Identification

Though stores sign an agreement to use the manufacturer's name or trade name and/or yarn identification, their ads will sometimes fail to include one or both names.

The sales manager must again determine whether to allow the ad, compromise the amount, or disallow the grant.

If the amount is large, a disallowance could create a serious situation between the buyer and the merchandise manager or controller, as buyers are suppoed to approve the copy.

In any event, a letter should be sent to the buyer and advertising manager calling to their attention the failure to properly list the names agreed upon and warning them that any further failure to do so will result in a rejection of the debit memo.

Ads Based on Volume

Stores planning a special supplement, mailer, or catalog will request a dollar amount which may exceed the normal grant.

They may agree to use a larger than normal quota of goods. This quota may be allotted in specific amounts to each store, and if anticipated sales are not realized, the result will be a disallowance for the stores concerned. Or, the stores may agree to a percentage of the total grant if anticipated sales are not realized.

Such special arrangements are often facilitated by reducing salesmen's commissions; this may be necessary to obtain the order.

Overpricing

This arrangement to increase the advertising budget does not require an accompanying ad or agreement, as the store is spending its own money.

However, the claim clerk is sent an allowance form or advertising form so that proper credit may be issued when the claim is received.

Combination of Overpricing and Ad Grant

This arrangement requires an advertising grant form and a price allowance.

Unspent Ad Grant

Experience has taught the authors that from 10 to 15 percent of all advertising grants are not used. Therefore the sales manager may safely allow advertising grants in excess of 10 percent of the budgeted figure.

Deferred Grants

Some—but few—large stores that do not spend the grant during the season for which it was intended arrange to spend it the following season, usually for a costly ad.

Radio and Television

The debit memo for radio and television advertising is usually supported by bills from the station, programs, or summaries of the scripts.

Indirect Advertising

Dollar grants for indirect advertising, such as for new-store openings (usually institutional), modeling, door prizes, gifts to sales personnel, and contests, are arranged specifically for that purpose and do not require substantiation.

Summary

At the end of a season or year the claim clerk makes a list of the grants for each store, the volume shipped, and the ratio of dollars to volume. These figures are entered on a yearly progress report form to evaluate if the amounts granted are producing increased volume.

chapter nine

SAMPLE LETTERS AND FORMS

HOW TO HANDLE CLAIMS

Letter A (page 5)

Dear __________:

We wrote to you on _____, having previously
(date)

written to you on _____
(date)

We have not received a reply to either of these letters, and we would appreciate a response so that we can bring this matter to a satisfactory conclusion.

Unless we hear from you within a reasonable period, we shall be forced to take up this matter with your controller.

We trust therefore that we shall hear from you by return mail.

Yours truly,

Letter B (page 5)

To the Controller:

We regret the necessity of enlisting your good services in resolving a claim made by your store under debit memo number ____, a copy of which we are enclosing.

We have written to your accounts payable division a number of times, as per the enclosed copies, and have failed to receive any response.

We will appreciate your efforts in trying to bring this matter to an early conclusion.

Yours truly,

PRICES

Letter A (page 15)

Dear ________:

We are in receipt of your debit memo number ____ claiming that the price on style number ____ was billed incorrectly at ____ per dozen.

We are enclosing a copy of your order, together with the nearest price and delivery schedule showing that the price billed to you was our regular price at the time your order was placed.

We are therefore voiding your debit memo by rebilling the amount to you, and we will appreciate your marking your records accordingly.

Yours truly,

CONSPIRACY

Letter (page 25)

Attention of Controller:

We have been plagued by tremendous shortage claims from you over the past few weeks.

We previously received large shortage claims, and so it became necessary to have our plant manager personally recheck each shipment before it left our premises. Despite this fact, we have received in the past few weeks three additional large shortage claims as follows:

(List same)

We are herewith enclosing letters from our plant manager regarding these claims and showing that the contents' weights that he verified were in accordance with the weights on file. Having rechecked these shipments prior to leaving our distribution plant, having received a proper receipt from the receiving carrier, and having determined that all the cartons were signed for by you in good order, we can only believe that these shortages do not exist and that this is an internal problem in your organization.

You can readily see that there is something wrong and that the matter bears investigation. At this point your account is unprofitable to us.

We are not sending a copy of this letter to your buyers or to __________, whose name appears on the claim slips, or to __________, the checker, or to the accounts payable division, as you may want to institute an investigation without their knowledge.

Thank you for your prompt advice.

Yours truly,

SHORTAGES

Letter (page 26)

To the Controller:

We regret the necessity of bringing to your attention the receipt by us of numerous shortage claims on practically every shipment made to you. Copies of the claims are enclosed.

We have verified the weights and have determined that no shortage should exist.

We have serviced your company for many years as we do almost every major department store in your area, without receiving any appreciable claims for shortages.

We have written to your accounts payable division as well as to your receiving manager a number of times, as per the enclosed copies of letters, but to no avail.

We feel that this is an internal matter in your organization and that it bears investigation. These are all small claims, and if they were isolated claims we would honor them and credit your company.

We will appreciate your cooperation in investigating this matter.

Yours truly,

TRANSPORTATION

Letter A (page 30)

Dear ___________:

We are in receipt of your claim and penalty charge for failure to combine in one shipment two different shipments received by you on the same day.

Shipments leave our distribution plant when packed at different times of the day. Shipments for different orders may be handled at different times and by different packers during the day.

Shipments may leave our distribution plant on different days and may arrive at your location on the same day.

These are conditions beyond our control, and we therefore cannot honor your claim and penalty charge. We are rebilling these charges to you.

Yours truly,

Letter B (page 30)

Dear _______________:

We cannot honor any claim because orders for different divisions were shipped on the same date under different bills of lading.

Shipments leave our distribution plant when packed at different times of the day. Shipments for different orders may be handled at different times and by different packers during the day.

Shipments may leave our distribution plant on different days and may arrive at your location on the same day.

In addition, orders for different divisions may be handled by different pickers and packers, and we have not agreed—and will not agree—to combine such shipments made on the same date.

We are therefore declining your claim and penalty charge and will rebill the charge to you.

Yours truly,

CONCEALED LOSS AND DAMAGE CLAIM

Letter (page 35)

Dear ________

We are in receipt of your debit memorandum number ______ in the amount of $ ______ covering a concealed shortage (or damage) claim.

Evidently you are not familiar with the laws and regulations covering this type of claim.

The general rule is that title to the merchandise shipped passes to the consignee upon delivery of such merchandise to the carrier for transportation to the destination.

Claims for shortages and damages must be filed against the carrier by the owner of the goods.

Prompt opening and checking of the shipment and prompt reporting of a concealed loss or damage as soon as it is discovered is required by the carrier if he is to make a voluntary refund for the loss or damage incurred.

The carrier should be informed by telephone and a request for an inspection confirmed by registered letter (return receipt requested) within forty-eight (48) hours to fifteen (15) days after receipt of the merchandise. Different carriers require different time limits within which to request an inspection. The consignee should determine from all the delivering carriers in his area the exact time limit within which he is required to request an inspection.

The consignee is also obligated to hold the containers and contents intact for such inspection.

Governmental regulations require the carrier to make the examination within a reasonable period.

Most carriers issue regulations (included on their form for claims for loss and damage) stating that they will make the inspection requested within five working days (excluding Saturdays, Sundays, and holidays). Other carriers do not specify the exact number of days within which they will make an inspection.

Again, it is best to determine from all delivering carriers in your area the exact number of days within which they will make an inspection.

Inasmuch as the consignee is required to keep the containers and merchandise intact awaiting an inspection, the waiting period in accordance with governmental regulations must be a reasonable one.

If the carrier fails to make a timely inspection, the consignee may make his own written inspection, which shall be considered a carrier's inspection report and will not unduly affect the consignee's recovery.

If you have observed the above regulations, your claim against us should be canceled since, as explained above, it properly should be made against the carrier.

If you have not requested a timely inspection, then you are barred from obtaining any voluntary settlement from the carrier.

In either event your claim against us should be canceled. We will gladly render to you any assistance or provide any documents you may require in order to substantiate your claim.

Yours truly,

Letter (page 40)

Dear ________ :

We find that the first notification we have of a substantial shortage is a deduction from a remittance to us in which you list your debit memo number for $____.

You deducted the amount of the above debit memo from your check number ____, dated ____, in the amount of $ ____. This necessitated our writing to you for a copy of the debit memo, which we received on ____.
(date)

When you realize that this shipment was made on ____ *(date)* and that we received the first detailed notice of a shortage of this size four months after the shipment was made, you should understand the problems you have created for both of us.

If you have a concealed loss claim it is barred because, in accordance with regulations, an inspection should have been requested within forty-eight (48) hours or fifteen (15) days (depending on the delivering carrier) after receipt of the goods.

You must now first advise us how many cartons you received, as it is evident from the size of your claim that either straggling cartons were received at a later date, and the claim was not reversed by you, or the truckman failed to deliver some of the cartons.

A tracer four months later takes twice as long as a tracer made immediately after the shortage is discovered.

While we are asking you for the above information and requesting the carrier to prove delivery, because of the length of time since the delivery we must disclaim responsibility for this loss. Under ICC regulations the shipment, once put into the hands of a common carrier, becomes your property, and it is necessary for you as the consignee to file the claim against the carrier.

Please advise us as promptly as possible, giving us the necessary information, and we will do our best to trace the shipment and request proof of delivery.

Yours truly,

TO: ______________________ REFERENCE TO DATE: __________

______________________ OUR P. O. NUMBER: __________

______________________ YOUR INVOICE NUMBER: __________

Gentlemen:

We have just received a shipment in violation of our shipping instructions as checked below. This violation will result in a chage-back to you, per our previous warning letter.

______Shipment before date specified on purchase order.

______Shipment after automatic cancellation date on order.

______Shipments for different stores not packed separately as instructed.

______Unauthorized partial shipment.

______Department number and order number not on each carton.

______Shipments on same order for different stores not combined.

______Shipment via unauthorized carrier.

______Packing slip or invoice not in carton.

______Stores not invoiced separately.

______Two or more purchase orders per invoice.

______Department number and order number not on invoice.

______Overage, shortage, or unauthorized substitution of merchandise.

Remember, your shipping violations incur additional costs and delays in processing your merchandise. Please adhere to our shipping instructions to avoid further charge-backs.

COMMENTS: ____

____

____

Sincerely,

Traffic Manager

(See paragraph titled Penalty Charges on page 7.)

chapter ten

HANDLING OF RETURNS

Percentage of Volume

Returns from customers are an inescapable part of doing business, and if returns are in excess of 1 percent of the annual volume, they can prove burdensome and harmful to the profits and working capital of a business.

Returns of 1/2 of 1 percent are considered reasonable.

Special situations of a few unusually large returns can distort the percentage figure.

There will always be borderline cases, where those doing an inspection must judge whether to classify a product as a first or a second. If the buyers or consumers subsequently grade it otherwise, and in sufficient numbers, then inspection grading may have to be tightened in order to reduce the number of returns.

Classification of Returns

The reason for returns generally falls into one of the following categories:

Faulty fabrics
Faulty fabrics—latent defects
Faulty factory work
Sales department errors
Distribution plant errors
Customer's problems
Packaging errors
Transportation errors

The sales department can be helpful by forwarding to the return clerk all the necessary information for properly classifying a return. This information, fully explaining the reason for the return, should be attached to the customer's debit memo.

Analysis of Returns

It is helpful to analyze the return so that management can study the causes and take corrective measures to reduce the most frequent type of return.

Much can be learned by the production manager, quality control manager, and the engineering staff if the claim clerk is instructed as to the reasons for returns. He should not only classify returns for resale but also correctly record them.

Weekly Reports

The return clerk sends to each division a weekly report listing under the style number the amount to be resold as firsts, seconds, thirds, and washed garments.

When first-quality styles are to be resold in large quantities, especially late in the season, then such information should be teletyped immediately.

The same procedure applies to returns of first-quality styles previously withdrawn from sale.

Monthly Reports

The return clerk keeps a continuing record of each return, listing the name and address of the customer, the style number, dozens, dollar amount, and the reason for the return.

The reasons are recorded in columns and the amount inserted under the applicable column. These columns are totaled for monthly comparison so that programs to reduce returns can be compared and progress to reduce them evaluated.

Return Clerk

The return clerk, if knowledgeable, will recognize if an unusual amount of returns is received for a particular style, pattern, or color and will note if the returns are for similar reasons. He will promptly alert management to the situation. Stock on hand can then be reexamined either for reclassification or because of a possible claim against the resource.

Changes and adjustments may be necessary to prevent a recurrence of the cycle of shipments and returns. The return clerk may request inspection by quality control to reexamine marginal returns for proper classification for resale.

Index Cards

The claim clerk in the accounting department receives a copy of the monthly report and should use it to update the customer's index card by showing the date and dollar amount of unjustified returns. (See form on page 125.)

If too many unjustified returns are received from an account, the account is then reviewed with the sales manager.

Few Defective—Entire Stock Returned

Stores which receive an abnormal amount of returns from customers of a particular style, size, or color may return the entire balance of their stock, as they fear the sale-return cycle.

It is best to accept the return. As the reason is generally given in this instance, the return clerk should be warned, and a careful inspection of the return and stock becomes mandatory.

Recognizing Style Number

The return clerk should have a numerically listed style number book and also a corresponding swatch of the fabric, a description of the style, and the selling price.

Often returns are received with the style number ticket illegible or missing, and then identification, especially of prior seasons' styles, is difficult.

Garment Not Manufactured by Your Company

Garments may be returned, either without a style ticket or with a debit memo listing your style number. An examination and the style number book may indicate that the garment was not manufactured by your company.

A return sticker should be requested and an invoice sent to the customer. The invoice should list the debit memo and any delivery charges thereon, together with any return transportation charges.

It is preferable to send an invoice rather than request a credit memo to cancel the incorrect debit memo. The reason is that it takes too long to receive a credit memo and repayment, whereas an invoice under "net cash terms" will be paid at a much earlier date. Also, redelivery charges are easier to collect by this method.

If the customer is one which has been assessing penalty charges, then a penalty charge should be added to the invoice.

Out-of-Country Returns

Out-of-country returns are the most difficult to handle because of duties, the length of time involved in receiving the return, minimum-weight problems, and costly transportation charges.

If goods are allegedly damaged, an attempt should be made to avoid the return by granting an allowance so that the customer may sell the garment as a second without loss to him.

The same theory should be applied when a return is requested because of a faulty delivery by the manufacturer, be it lateness or incorrect style, sizing, colors, etc. It is preferable to make a reasonable allowance in order to prevent the return.

Product Sold at Different Prices

Slow-moving styles may be marked down in price, and dates of such markdowns should be recorded.

The return clerk should endeavor to apply the return to the proper invoice and to the proper salesman's commission. This is not always easily accomplished, but it is worth the effort.

Credit Withdrawn

After credit approval has previously been given, a credit man may become aware of a customer's financial difficulties, resulting in chapter 10 or 11 bankruptcy proceedings, collection suits, checks returned due to insufficient funds, extreme lateness in payments, etc. Instructions to stop additional shipments are Teletyped, and some shipments may be stopped and recalled and credited.

Product Insurance

Latent defects are a number of conditions that may develop later and that may affect the consumer—conditions such as flammability and tendencies to cause skin diseases and aggravate allergies.

Return of the balance of the stock is always accepted. Such offending styles should be withdrawn from sale until tests have been made by a qualified laboratory to determine if it is safe to release the stock for continued sales.

It is surprising to learn of the many companies which do not carry product insurance. Considering the large awards being given by juries, carrying such insurance is mandatory.

Consequential Damage

Fabric defects may affect other garments, furniture, and accessories.

Fabric resource contracts outlaw recovery of any consequential damage. The garment manufacturer therefore is not protected unless he can obtain coverage under a liability or product liability policy.

Authorized Returns

Most order forms, catalogs, packing slips, and invoices notify the customer that only authorized returns to a directed address will be accepted. These items require the customer to request a return sticker (gummed) which must be placed on the return container in order to be accepted by the resource's distribution plant.

The customer should provide the style number, amount to be returned, and the reason for the return.

Return Sticker

Return stickers should be in duplicate and should have consecutive numbers. (See form on page 123.)

One copy is sent to the customer to be attached to the container. Thc duplicate is attached to the customer's debit memo or request and forwarded to the return clerk.

The return clerk should notify the sales department if the actual return materially differs from what is indicated on the return sticker.

Insurance on Return Sticker

Though most companies carry a floater policy on transportation, they are reluctant to make small claims against the insurance company, reserving the use of the policy for larger and more meaningful claims. Therefore, the return sticker should contain authorization for the customer to insure the return, especially if the transportation method and rate (such as $50 on express shipments) do not cover the full dollar amount of the return.

Routing on Returns

Stores often route returns, especially low-weight returns, in a manner that carries a minimum-weight rate, such as via truck at a minimum weight of 100 pounds when the return only weighs 10 to 20 pounds.

This results in a charge almost triple that of the charge for returning the same shipment via parcel post or United Parcel Service (UPS).

Such overcharges are difficult to recover from customers. The return sticker should specify the method and routing to be employed.

This is very important on large returns, especially late in the season when any delay caused by an incorrect routing could lead to a markdown. The return may be received so late that it cannot be shipped at regular prices.

Debit Memos on Returns

Return stickers should also carry a request that customers are to include a debit memo covering the return.

Debit memos should include the following information:

Debit memo number
Customer's order number
Customer's department number
Resource invoice number
Number of containers in return
Routing of return
Transportation charges
Reason for return

This will not only be helpful in crediting the store for the proper amount but will also eliminate much unnecessary correspondence by both the accounts payable department of the customer and the accounts receivable department of the resource. Many stores enclose only packing slips. Therefore credits do not include any other charges such as for transportation. Often stores attach debit memos to their remittances, which may be received weeks or months after the return is received and credited. This invariably leads to unnecessary correspondence and the eventual issuance of an additional credit.

Unauthorized Returns

Some customers, especially large department stores and chains, make large returns without giving prior notice to either the sales department or the distribution plant. This causes unnecessary additional expense and effort on the part of all concerned:

The distribution plant must obtain permission from the sales department.

The truckman is kept waiting, or he will refuse to wait and will return the shipment to his terminal; this results in delivery, redelivery, and storage charges.

The sales department must contact the buyer by long-distance telephone, and the buyer is often unavailable.

The shipment may be accepted and not credited until the necessary approval is obtained; this results in lost sales and possible markdowns.

Thus, in the interest of an economical operation by both the customer and the shipper, and in the interest of a mutually cooperative relationship, such unauthorized returns should be eliminated, and proper procedures should be followed.

Refused Returns

Large, prestigious resources with national brands are taking a firm stance in this regard and are refusing unauthorized returns, regardless of the size of the customer. Medium-size and smaller resources are doing the same with smaller customers, but they are at a disadvantage with larger customers.

When shipments are refused, a certified letter (return receipt requested) should be sent to the customer detailing the circumstances and disavowing responsibility for the disposition of the merchandise and any additional delivery and storage charges. (See Letter A on page 116.)

In addition, the delivering carrier is required to notify both the shipper and the consignee that the undelivered goods are being held. The carrier must give the address at which the goods are being stored and request that it receive a disposition notice within fifteen days from the date of the on-hand notice.

If no disposition is advised within the fifteen-day period, one more notice giving fifteen additional days for final disposition is sent. If no disposition is advised within the second period, the carrier may then legally sell the merchandise at the best price obtainable in order to cover his delivery, redelivery, and storage charges. If the sum produced from the sale is insufficient to cover the carrier's charges, the carrier may recover from the owner any balance involved.

The word "owner" is important, for if the customer has not adhered to the terms on the order or invoice, he may well become the "owner."

In the interest of future relations, the resource should make every effort to resolve the matter before it reaches the stage of "sale for carrier's charges."

If necessary, the resource should communicate with the controller, especially if the resource is unable to resolve the matter with the accounting, merchandising, or shipping department of the customer. (See Letter B on page 116.)

Storage and redelivery charges are difficult to recover. Refusal of a shipment should be brought to the management's attention before attempting to recover such charges. If storage and redelivery charges are to be collected from the customer, it is best to rebill the customer rather than expect a credit memo or refund. In such instances, although the account is credited, no copy of the credit is mailed to the customer.

Many firms have, in light of their previous experiences, decided to never refuse a shipment but to accept the shipment and leave it unopened. They do not issue credit to the resource until the matter has been resolved, thus eliminating redelivery charges and storage charges. They avoid creating a difficult climate for the sales manager and the buyer while the matter is being resolved.

In all cases, the claim clerk must be notified so that the matter will appear in the follow-up cycle folder and not be allowed to remain unresolved for an unreasonable period.

Misdirected Returns

Returns are on occasion made to branch offices, showrooms, or general offices. In most instances there are no facilities to handle returns, especially if they are of considerable bulk.

This necessitates either rerouting at additional expense or refusing the return if the delivering carrier will not reroute.

Small shipments should be placed in a carton, and when full the carton should be returned to the distribution plant. Care must be taken to list each return by name of customer, address, and debit number if known so that in the event of a loss or damage the contents and value will be on record.

A form letter to the customer should be sent so that a possible recurrence of misdirected returns can be avoided. (See Letter A on page 118.)

Issuing Credit for Returns

On the theory that returns from customers, upon being signed for by a common carrier, are the property of the consignee, the customer's debit memo should be credited in full.

Once a debit memo is issued by a customer, the full amount of the debit memo is deducted from a subsequent payment. Refunds for any difference, be it for price, extension, transportation, or garments of another manufacturer, are difficult to collect, and many months can go by before an adjustment is made by the customer, if it is made at all.

All items that are incorrectly listed on the debit memo and credited, as explained above, should be invoiced back to the store and the credit and invoice cross-referred.

Consequently the customer will not be under the impression that you are allowing his debit memorandum in full. Many resources do not mail copies of their credits to the stores because they feel that the customer may deduct the credit as well as the amount on their own debit memo.

Copies of all invoices charging unallowed items back to the store should be sent to the claim clerk for follow-up.

Concealed Loss and Damage on Returns

Claims for concealed loss and damage on returns should be handled in the same manner as claims for concealed loss and damage on shipments to customers.

Missing Cartons or Entire Return

If a few cartons should be missing, or if the entire return has gone astray (the carrier being unable to prove delivery), an invoice should be made out charging the carrier for the missing quantity. The original copy is to be sent to the claim clerk for the purpose of filing a claim and for follow-up.

Seconds Not Returned

Large mail-order and retail chains have a policy of not returning individual garments returned by customers or found in stock as defective merchandise. Periodically, these accounts charge the resource 50 percent of the net selling price.

This procedure of working on the honor system, if not abused, saves both parties considerable effort in making the return. It saves billing, payments, transportation charges, inspection, re-pressing, grading, reselling, crediting, and reshipping.

chapter eleven

RETURNS DUE TO FABRIC DAMAGES

Theory

Fabric damages are divided into two categories: patent defects and latent defects.

Patent defects are defects which are apparent under reasonable examination.

Latent defects are defects which are present or may develop and which are not fairly visible or detectable under reasonable examination. (Latent defects are described elsewhere in this chapter.)

Patent defects are generally easily recognized, and the terms describing them have appeared in many publications.

Manufacturers generally cut out and remove such patent defects, and returns for patent defects are small in number.

Latent Defects

Latent defects are defects which are present or may develop and which are not fairly visible or detectable under reasonable examination.

Theory of Latent Defects

Returns due to latent defects can eventually present a serious and costly problem.

With the first inkling of a return due to a latent defect, management should immediately be concerned with the problem and make every effort to minimize the effect.

While only a few garments may be involved when the situation first arises, the problem may grow to sizable proportions.

Latent defects may become apparent while the stock is in the hands of the manufacturer, but they are usually recognized after a customer's complaint or return.

Notification to Fabric Supplier

Most fabric suppliers' confirmations limit the filing of claims for latent defects to a period of ninety days after shipment. Some confirmations read thirty or sixty days. These should be changed to ninety days before contracts are signed.

Most reputable fabric suppliers will stand behind their goods and not invoke the ninety-days clause. But if the claim is sizable, they might invoke the ninety-days clause.

Therefore when the garment manufacturer becomes aware of a latent defect, he should immediately notify the fabric supplier by registered mail. (See Letter B on page 122.)

Identification

Many garment manufacturers using more than one supplier of a particular fabric fail to put the cutting lot number on their size or trade labels.

It is becoming increasingly important to note cutting lot numbers, not only in the case of latent defects, but also for use in flammability suits or government inspections and for yarn identification.

When the lot number is known, the source of the goods is a matter of record.

Odor

This is one of the most common forms of a latent defect. The odor is obnoxious, generally caused by formaldehyde, which is used in the finishing of fabrics to produce a drip-dry, crease-resistant, or permanent press finish.

The problem of odor is more prevalent in the summer months and in areas where the temperature is high..

It may also be prevalent in garments enclosed in cellophane bags.

Formaldehyde makes the eyes tear, and it may cause employees to be absent frequently or even leave the employ of the company.

The odor may contaminate other garments or other fabrics.

It has proved difficult thus far to make the odor disappear once it has permeated the garment and area.

Odor has been known to affect as many as 25,000 garments in one establishment.

Various methods to remove odor have been tried by fabric resources, none of which have proved consistently and completely successful.

A well-known resource has developed a spray that removes the odor but replaces it with another odor, not as obnoxious, but still unacceptable.

Other resources have tried sachet bags, perfumes, laying the garments out in the sun, and leaving the garments exposed—all of which have proved unsuccessful and uneconomic.

The most successful method to date discovered by the writers is one that costs a fraction of a cent a garment.

It was tried on many thousands of garments which were shipped to customers, and not a single garment was returned because of odor.

The method did not change the shade, fabric, or finish and drys instantly.

The procedure was to place the garment on a hanger and apply a quick spray of Lysol disinfectant to the front and back and one quick burst to the inside.

The disinfectant was sprayed from a distance of about 18 inches so that the garment was not wetted.

The garment was left to dry a few minutes and was available for shipment shortly thereafter.

Sublimation

Sublimation is the transfer of color from the fabric of the garment to another article.

It is a form of crocking, except that the transfer is made by contact and not by rubbing, as is the case in crocking.

Sublimation rarely occurs, and when it does the fabric usually contains acetate or some form of acetate.

The color in the garment will discolor the tissue used in the packing of the carton, the hang-tag, the label, and cardboards.

As soon as such a situation is noticed, the receiving clerk should notify quality control so that garments in stock may be examined to see if there is discoloration of the labels and hang-tags of that style and other styles of the same fabric as well as adjoining garments.

The fabric purchaser should also be informed so that the fabric resource can be notified. (See Letter B on page 122.)

If garments in stock are affected by sublimation, they should be isolated for treatment as described below. Once having been affected by sublimation, garments will not sublimate again.

Garments affected by sublimation should be repacked with fresh tissue in a fresh carton, and the carton should be sealed and allowed to remain sealed for a week. Labels and tags should previously have been replaced.

After the carton has been reopened and no further sublimation is noticed, then the garments can be reshipped, especially to smaller accounts, without much chance of another return due to sublimation.

The resource generally is willing to pay for any extra expenses involved, such as for inward and outward transportation and labor.

If sublimation recurs, then garments will either have to again be repacked to see if sublimation finally disappears or sold as seconds, with the charge to the resource increased by the loss in sales as irregulars.

Tests for sublimation can be made by placing garments together for four hours at 220° Fahrenheit under dry and moist heat.

Migration

As with sublimation, migration in most cases is found in garments made of acetate yarns.

There is no present explanation of why migration occurs, nor has a method been discovered to predetermine if it will occur.

Migration is the transfer of color from one garment to another in an irregular pattern, and it can occur not only between two garments in contact but also between one garment and another one a short distance away.

Garments affected by migration cannot be redeemed. Depending upon the extent of the color transfer, they are classified as seconds or thirds, and they may be so unsightly as to be a complete loss.

Chemical Reaction

Certain metallic trims made with metallic yarns, especially on acetate fabrics, contain special finishes to make them firm enough to go easily through a folder.

These trims may cause a chemical reaction in which the outline of the metallic trim (usually a braid) transfers to another garment touching the trim, either in stock or in the shipping container.

As in migration, garments so affected are graded seconds, thirds, or unsalable.

The garment manufacturer should supply the trim resource with samples of the fabric and matching trim so that they can be tested, usually with extreme heat, to see if such a reaction will occur.

Water finishes on metallic trims, instead of oil or chemical finishes, have been successful in firming trims without producing a chemical reaction.

Fastness to Light (Fluorescent)

Certain bright colors, when in vogue, can only be produced by fluorescent shades, and most mills when using fluorescent shades bar any claims for light fastness. Light fastness is a latent defect, as the discoloration and loss of shade and brightness occur most often after the garments have been manufactured.

Loss of shade and depth of color may be uneven, and returns due to this defect must be accepted without the manufacturer making any recovery for the loss from the resource, if the resource's shade card or confirmation specifies that no claims will be accepted.

If the resource fails to bar claims on color or shade cards and confirmations, then a claim may be entered because of returns due to light fastness of fluorescent dyes.

Fastness to Light (Phototropic)

Certain shades, usually of the fluorescent group of dyes, may be phototropic; that is, if high and bright shades are exposed to light, there will be a change in shade. The original shade returns when the garment is placed in a dark room. This treatment may or may not then result in shading or shade variation.

Fastness to Light Bulb or Sun Exposure

Garments that are not boxed and that are placed too near a light bulb for too long a period of time will show shading at the point nearest the bulb. Returns due to this defect may be refused.

Garments in store windows, exposed to the sun, will often show shading discolorations. As single garments are usually involved, returns are generally accepted.

Allergies and Skin Disease

With the advent of so many new yarns, finishes, and dyes, many of them not completely perfected, there is an increase in claims concerning skin disease, rashes, etc. Many people with allergies are entering complaints and filing suits; they claim damages because of adverse reactions affecting their skin and health.

Stores become frightened when such complaints appear, and they return the entire stock of the style or color concerned.

Little can be done to persuade the stores that adverse reactions to fabrics are isolated situations. Generally the resource is fighting a losing battle in trying to bar the returns.

Product insurance is a prime necessity for the garment manufacturer.

Washability

Washability is generally not considered under latent defects. Most garments will perform satisfactorily if washed properly in accordance with instructions.

With the advent of "care labeling," returns due to washability should decrease.

With so many hundreds of millions of garments being washed, and with so many detergents and bleaches on the market, garments will continue to be washed improperly.

Most stores have the policy of accepting returns of this nature without discussion, and they expect the supplier to have a similar policy. This kind of return is just another expense of doing business.

The return clerk should alert management if an unusual number of garments of the same style, print, pattern, or color are returned because of problems regarding washability, because if many are received in the same category, the stock should be inspected and tested.

Flammability

Standards of flammability will, as time goes on, increase so that eventually regulations will cover all fabrics, except outerwear and certain industrial fabrics. The details of existing regulations have been widely published, and this chapter concerns itself only with the nontechnical requirements for the protection against claims and the handling of claims.

Because the awards granted by juries have been known to exceed $500,000, it is important that each purchaser of fabrics and each manufacturer of fabrics and garments obtain *Product Liability Insurance* in an amount of not less than $1 million so as to be protected against claims for multiple injuries and deaths arising out of a single incident.

Each invoice should contain the following:

> Based upon a guaranty received, the undersigned hereby guarantees that reasonable and representative tests, made according to the procedures prescribed in section 4(a) of the Flammable Fabrics Act, show that fabrics used or contained in the articles of wearing apparel and fabrics otherwise subject to such act, covered by and in the form delivered under this document, are not, under the provisions of such act, so highly flammable as to be dangerous when worn by individuals.

Purchasers of fabrics should obtain a continuing guarantee from their resources, in the language prescribed in the Flammable Fabrics Act. The continuing guarantee should cover a period of three years from the date of the guarantee. The expiration date of the guarantee should be recorded and heeded so that a new continuing guarantee is received prior to the expiration of the current one.

Though the Flammable Fabrics Act requires that records

be kept for a period of three years, it is advisable to keep records for at least the length of time specified in the statute of limitations, or for as many as ten years. Judges have been known to permit suits to be filed and tried, in the case of injury to minors, when the minors' interests were not properly protected.

Samples of each color and lot of fabric, purchase records, and process sheets should be maintained for the same period. If the samples are maintained, new tests may be made and may be of considerable weight in proving that the fabrics were tested properly and were approved in accordance with the required standards.

As soon as a summons is served, your attorney should be notified. He in turn should immediately notify your insurance company by registered letter.

As soon as the garment or fabric can be identified, all samples and records should be sought so that the suppliers' names can be furnished to your attorney and insurance company.

Full cooperation should be given to your insurance company so as to minimize any judgments against them and to ensure a reasonable premium for continued coverage.

All conversations with the plaintiffs and codefendants should be conducted solely through your attorney or insurance company.

chapter twelve

RETURNS DUE TO MANUFACTURING DAMAGES

Theory

Like fabric damages, manufacturing defects are generally easily recognized, as the terms describing them have appeared in many publications.

Industrial Engineering

In addition, unlike fabric manufacturers, most sizable manufacturers of garments have an industrial engineering staff or engineering consultants who are in constant or weekly attendance to see that garments are produced properly and economically.

Nevertheless, there is a higher percentage of returns due to faulty manufacturing than for any other reason.

This is understandable when one realizes that as many as

fifty or more individual operators perform some portion of the work required in the manufacturing of a single garment.

Floor ladies and management, as well as the engineering staff, constantly monitor the quality of the work during the sewing operation so that any faulty work can be detected and repaired while still at the sewing stage.

Inspection

When the garment has been completed, it is again inspected by quality control people, and again there will be borderline cases in which their judgment must prevail.

Many manufacturers, in cases where the garment construction permits it, are inserting the inspectors' numbers in order to tighten quality control inspection and to keep track of all returns due to faulty fabric or manufacturing defects passed by individual inspectors.

The location of the defect is important in deciding whether the garment is a first, second, or third. A defect under the collar or arm should be classified differently from one on the front, collar, or pocket.

Classification of Manufacturing Defects

Manufacturing defects and items subject to defects are listed below for the purpose of classification of returns, if management desires such information in order to minimize future returns due to manufacturing defects:

Buttons, gripper	Alignment
Inspection	Measurements and specifications
Missing	Buttons, snaps, belts, accessories, care labels, tags
Mixing bundles	Shading, trim, sizing, measurements, labeling
Pressing	Facings, hems, collars, seams, pockets
Quilting	Hanging linings, creases, stitching
Sewing	Uneven collars, pockets, fronts, hems, and facings

Spots	Oil, grease, stains, dirt
Spreading / *Cutting* }	Shading, measurements, notches, holes, pencil marks
Trim	Shirring, laces, sewing, embroidery, bias, cording
Trimming	Hanging threads

Missing Articles

A store will write advising that a button, snap, or accessory is missing.

This should be given immediate attention and a letter of acknowledgment sent so that the store will be aware that the missing component will be forwarded. (See Letter C on page 122.)

Failure to notify the store may cause an unnecessary return.

chapter thirteen

RETURNS DUE TO DISTRIBUTION PLANT ERRORS

Theory

The opportunities of a distribution plant to make errors causing customers' returns are many. It is surprising that so few returns are due solely to errors of the distribution plant.

A manufacturer servicing the department store and specialty store trade may very well sell to 4,000 or more accounts.

Department stores issue confirmations which may or may not be attached to the salesman's order when it arrives at the distribution plant.

With the ever-growing number of branches and distribution centers for the major department stores, the problems of the resources' shipping centers have considerably increased.

Almost each major store's confirmation has clauses unique to the store, and many confirmations are in such fine print that they are difficult to read and decipher.

It would be of inestimable help and would contribute greatly to decreasing the cost of distribution centers of both stores and resources if a uniform purchase order could be adopted by the stores' trade organizations. A uniform purchase order would also contribute greatly to a more systematic handling of orders and would help decrease returns due to errors on the part of the distribution centers as well as the sales department.

Despite data processing, distribution plants do have to merchandise their inventories.

Fabrics are not always received from fabric suppliers in the color proportions ordered.

Sewing plants will make irregulars, and if the irregulars are mostly in one color the stock assortment will be less than ideal.

Therefore stores do not always receive an assortment exactly as ordered—especially late in the season when recuts are not planned.

Most stores understand this, but there is a minority that does not, and these stores remain constant returners. These accounts may be reviewed as to their profitability to the resource.

Below are listed the most frequent reasons for returns due to distribution plant errors.

Duplicate Shipments

A style may be shipped twice because the original order was not marked showing that the style was already shipped. A return usually results.

Labels

Certain styles are made exclusively for "group purchasers" (usually through buying offices).

There may remain an unsold portion of the total quantity that has to be sold through the regular sales force.

The private labels must be removed and regular labels inserted. Such changes must be done with dexterity so as to avoid returns.

Colors

Shipments of too many of one color in relation to the other colors will result in returns.

Late Shipments

Orders from large stores have a shipping date as well as a cancellation date.

Orders from small stores also have a shipping date, but often the salesman will insert the cancellation date without the store's agreement. If business is off and stocks remain high, the small stores may refuse the shipment. (Refusals are discussed in the chapter "Returns Due to Transportation Problems.")

Sizing

The sewing operator may insert the wrong size label in error, and this may be the cause of a warranted return.

Mismatching

In a two-piece garment, the sizes may, through error, be mismatched (for example, a 36 top and a 34 bottom). This usually results in a return to the store and then to the resource.

Automatic Cancellation

Many large stores have an automatic cancellation policy. Receiving departments are instructed to return all shipments made after the cancellation date.

The customer's index card should be marked to indicate that the store will return shipments made after the automatic cancellation date. (See form on page 126.)

Salvaging Late Shipments

If the distribution plant advises the sales manager of an anticipated late shipment, especially of a large quantity to a major store, the sales manager then has the opportunity to call the buyer and obtain an extension.

When such an extension is agreed to by the buyer, a notation of it should appear on the invoice.

Air Shipment

Often a sales manager will authorize a prepaid air shipment of a late delivery and will charge the store only the regular transportation rate.

The air shipment may make up for lost time so that the goods will arrive on time at the store.

In some instances, the sales manager will call the buyer, especially when goods are required for planned ads, and advise of such action.

When air shipments are made, they should be noted on the invoice, and the store should be advised that it is only being charged the regular transportation rate.

When the buyer's consent is also obtained, this also should be noted on the invoice and the buyer's name listed.

Shipments That Are Too Early

Large stores have "open to buy" budgets, and buyers plan their purchase orders so that invoice dollar amounts will not exceed the budgeted figures.

If shipments are made in advance of the scheduled shipping date, the amount of the invoice may exceed the budgeted figure, and the store may be obligated to return the shipment.

Advancing the due date or changing the invoice date is usually not satisfactory to the store, inasmuch as the receiving date is the controlling factor.

The distribution plant should be advised of this reason for a return so that it may hold the shipment intact for a later shipping date.

If the period before redelivery is a short one, arrangements may be made with the delivering carrier to warehouse the goods so as to minimize inward and outward transportation charges.

If there will be a long period before redelivery, the return may have to be re-pressed before reshipment.

Incorrect Style Shipped

The distribution plant may pick and ship a wrong style; for example, style 1003 instead of 1008. This is a human error and should not happen too often.

The distribution plant should make a replacement promptly as soon as it is advised of the error, and it should not wait for receipt of the incorrect style before making the replacement.

The distribution plant should not avoid rebilling and crediting, for once a debit memo is made out by the store, a deduction will follow. The resource will not receive payment for the replacement without actual billing.

Undershipment or Overshipment

Customers may notify the resource in a debit memo or letter of an overshipment of a style and of an undershipment of another style.

If there is a sizable shortage due to this kind of error, then the plant should be requested to check its records for verification.

If the dollar amount involved is nominal, then the customer's credit or debit memo should be accepted as rendered.

chapter fourteen

RETURNS DUE TO SHOW-ROOM ERRORS

Theory

Show rooms are generally located in major cities, where there is a high rate of turnover of show-room office personnel.

As a result, it is difficult to avoid the errors of duplication and checking of delivery dates that contribute to returns.

Confirmations and Duplicate Orders

Show-room clerks do not always recognize store confirmations as confirming an order previously sent to the distribution plant. They therefore write up another order, and this results in a double shipment.

Salesmen receive a copy of every order that their main office writes, and they should alert the show room to such duplication.

Confirmations are not always for the entire original order.

Therefore, if the part of the order that is not confirmed is not detected and canceled and is instead sent to the store, it will be considered an overshipment by the store, and a return will result.

Unconfirmed Orders

Unconfirmed orders should not be sent to the distribution center with an order number. This will ensure that the order will not be shipped without the actual confirmation on hand.

Distribution clerks, seeing an order number, assume that the order has been confirmed, and they may make a shipment that in all probability will be returned.

Hold for Store Breakdown

The same rule applies to orders marked "wait for store breakdown." While there is little possibility of such an order being prematurely shipped, it is best to have a uniform system whereby orders for large stores cannot be shipped without an order number.

Seasonal Accounts

Accounts in resort areas such as Florida or in mountain skiing areas may be open only during a seasonal period.

Salesmen, in order to avoid refusals and failure-to-deliver returns, should carefully mark their orders "Do not ship earlier than . . ." or "Do not ship after. . . ."

Delivery Schedule

Orders are booked in accordance with the open-to-sell delivery schedules. Such schedules should be mailed each Wednesday to ensure their arrival at the salesman's home or the place indicated on his route list over the weekend.

Orders booked for too early a delivery date that cannot be met invite returns due to late delivery.

Show-room clerks should send "date revision cards" when orders are received and delivery dates cannot be met. (See form on page 124.)

Automatic Credit Approval

Changes are constantly being made in automatically approved credit lists. A revision should be made as soon as notice of a change is received in order to avoid having the show room Teletype credit-approved orders for accounts that have been removed from the credit list.

This procedure will minimize attempts to recall shipments in transit that have not been approved.

Abbreviations

Show-room clerks should insist on and mark all orders with local street addresses and avoid abbreviations of cities and states.

In the same city there are stores with similar names, and if a shipment is delivered to the wrong consignee, it may take weeks or longer to determine where the shipment is.

When the shipment is finally traced, it may be too late for the customer's requirements, and a return may result.

When a state has two cities of the same name, then the proper county of the state should be listed. There is a space on the bill of lading for the insertion of the name of the county.

Cancellations

Cancellations, when received, should be Teletyped immediately to prevent any shipments from being made. It must be remembered that the customer may have mailed the cancellation two to five days earlier and assumed that no further shipments would be made.

If a resource's policy is to accept cancellations on open-line styles (not special orders), then it is best not to make additional shipments because refusals and returns result.

When a customer endeavors to return goods shipped between the time the store mails the cancellation notice and the time it is received by the resource, then a phone call or letter explaining the circumstances may result in an accepted shipment. (See Letter A on page 121.)

chapter fifteen

RETURNS DUE TO CUSTOMER PROBLEMS

Theory

Many returns are due to the individual problems of the customers and are not due to either faulty garments or any error on the part of the manufacturer.

Budget

Buyers work on budgets and are constantly being prodded by their merchandise managers regarding markup, turnover, inventory liquidity, increases in sales, and advertising cooperation.

As a result, buyers exert pressure on their resources to assist them in conforming with the above matters.

Many returns, especially from larger stores, are accepted because of the desire of the suppliers to maintain a good relationship with the larger stores, which provide them with a large volume of their business.

Because of the pressure from the merchandise managers and controllers, there are each year an increasing number of buyer changes. This in itself presents many problems to the resource in its attempt to increase sales, which is almost mandatory in the present era of ever-increasing inflationary costs of doing business.

Merchandise Manager

In the interest of increasing sales, sales managers should become acquainted with the store merchandise managers and maintain good relations and rapport with them. The support of the merchandise manager will be needed if the new buyer changes the buying pattern of the store, as this may seriously affect the manufacturer's volume with that particular store.

Change in Buyer

When a new buyer is appointed, he or she invariably finds fault with the predecessor's selection of styles; thus, existing orders are in jeopardy, and shipments en route may be refused.

There is no hard and fast rule that can be set. Each situation must be weighed as to the type and volume of the account and the relationship which exists.

If the resource expects to take back any goods, it is best to do so gracefully at the beginning and obtain as much goodwill as possible in order to cement the relationship with the store.

Sales managers should be aware of buyer changes and should get to know the new buyers. By quickly offering congratulations and cooperation, the sales manager may be able to prevent refusals, cancellations, or changes of existing orders.

Overselling

Some salesmen and sales managers almost merchandise the department for a buyer. They must be careful not to oversell, because when the salesman writes up the order himself he is making the selection of the style and quantity and may feel obliged to rescue the buyer if the expected sales do not materialize.

Quality Not Good Enough

The salesman will usually sell to anyone willing to buy, within the restrictions of the selling policy of the company.

He may sell to a store whose standards of quality are far higher than the standards required of the price line being offered.

It is best to accept the return and to instruct the salesman not to solicit the account in the future. The credit clerk's card should also be marked accordingly. (See form on page 125.)

Chronic Returners

Some stores are soon recognized as constant and chronic returners. The credit clerk's cards should be marked when there are unjustified returns, and if these returns continue, the salesmen should be instructed to refrain from soliciting any orders from these accounts.

Claim Because Style Was Not Ordered

A request for a return may be made because the customer claims the style was not ordered. Usually a copy of the order, preferably signed by the account, may induce the customer to retain the merchandise. (See Letter B on page 121.)

Ads That Don't Sell

A buyer planning an advertisement may overbuy to support the ad. If the ad does not pull enough sales as expected, the buyer will be under pressure to return a portion of the goods.

The buyer may have at the same time requested back-up

"unconfirmed orders." These unconfirmed orders should immediately be canceled so as to unfreeze the stock and make it available for shipment to others.

Markdown Money

When a return appears to be the only solution to satisfy the buyer, paying or sharing markdown money may be suggested so that the store may reduce the selling price. This is especially advisable toward the end of the season, when any returned goods may have to be marked down in the normal pattern of seasonal markdowns.

Open to Buy

Ads that don't pull and other styles that don't sell may freeze the buyer's "open to buy" money. The buyer may then try to arrange a return to be credited, thus increasing his ability to buy fresh seasonal merchandise. The buyer will at the same time issue a new order for the returned merchandise, specifying that it be shipped at a later date, usually the beginning of the next season for that type of merchandise.

Such cooperation with the buyer is generally appreciated and should result in an increasing volume of business.

Prepaid Return

A return made to accommodate an account should be made prepaid without any charge for inward transportation.

Some shipping departments of stores disregard this understanding and charge both inward and outward transportation. An invoice to the attention of the buyer should result in a refund of such charges.

Prompt Return

When a resource agrees to accept a return as an accommodation to the store, the return should be made as promptly as possible so that the goods can be made quickly available for resale and shipment to others.

When branch stores are involved, the buyer must be impressed with the necessity of gathering the goods so that the store's distribution center may be able to make the return in accordance with store policy.

It may be advisable to inform the store of the routing to be employed in order to ensure the quickest possible return.

Competitive Underselling

A store will occasionally complain that another store in town is selling the goods at a lower price, even though the resource sold the goods to both stores at the same price.

The resource must be careful not to violate the Robinson-Patman law, which prohibits conspiring with a buyer not to sell to the buyer's competitor.

The resource may agree to accept the return of the style being sold at a lower price, and it may judiciously sell different styles to each of the stores in the future.

chapter sixteen

RETURNS DUE TO PACKAGING ERRORS

Dirty Hems

Long garments, if not handled properly, may be received with the hems dirty.

They may have been hung on too low a rack, or during picking and packing they may have been carried with the hem dragging on the floor.

Staples

When automatic stapling machines are used, the staples may penetrate the carton and make holes in the garments.

Tissues

Tissues may be omitted or placed improperly, resulting in creases which are difficult to iron out.

Parcel Post Shipments

Postal clerks often toss packages, and this frequently results in torn and open ends—and damaged garments.

Rusty Pins

Pins that are in goods which are in stock too long or near damp areas may become rusty and discolor the garment. Such rust stains are difficult to remove.

Missing Accessories

Belts, ties, bows, and other accessories may be left off garments. If the store requests the missing items, such requests should be promptly acknowledged and the accessories sent to prevent a return. (See Letter C on page 122.)

Gummed Tape

If gummed tape is not securely handled, it may develop an objectionable odor; also, loose tape may be the cause of pilferage or damages to garments.

chapter seventeen

RETURNS DUE TO TRANSPORTATION PROBLEMS

Difficult and Controversial

Transportation presents the most difficult problems to the shipper as well as to the consignee.

There are three parties involved in every shipment: the shipper, the carriers, and the consignee. Of the three, only the carriers and their associations have made a serious and diligent effort to observe the laws, and they have issued pamphlets explaining the various rules that apply to shipping.

In an effort to improve their relationship with their customers, the carriers have set up regulations for their membership to more promptly and fairly resolve any differences with their customers. They have also provided a forum to which the shipper or consignee may appeal any differences with carriers in order to avoid serious and costly litigation.

Basic Rules and Laws

This chapter on returns due to transportation problems and the chapter on transportation claims are aimed to bring to the attention of the manufacturers and the stores the basic rules that cover most (but not all) claims regarding returns, damages, and shortages that apply to transportation.

If there is a fuller understanding of the rules and more cooperation between the manufacturers and the stores, problems that will continue to arise regarding transportation will be more fairly and expeditiously handled and resolved.

Ownership

Most of the misunderstandings are caused by the failure to know who is the "owner" of the goods.

The general rule is that title to merchandise shipped passes to the consignee upon the delivery of such merchandise to the carrier for transportation to a destination.

This rule, like practically every other rule, has exceptions. For example, when goods are sold "FOB store," title or ownership passes upon receipt of the goods by the consignee.

When goods are sold "freight prepaid," there can be difficulties if a claim is involved. If the intention is only to make a "freight allowance," goods should be sold "freight prepaid to destination, but FOB point of shipment."

The understanding of ownership is important, for it is the rule that the owner is the proper person to file claims for any loss or damage which is sustained during transportation.

While it is best for the owner to file the claim, the regulations do not preclude the shipper from doing so as the shipper generally does for large mail order companies.

Some of the possible exceptions as to the consignee being the owner are when goods sold FOB point of shipment are shipped after the cancellation date or when goods misdirected by the shipper arrive at the store after an unreasonable period following the cancellation date.

Acts of God

A carrier is not liable for loss of or injury to goods caused by an Act of God.

Acts of God include earthquakes, extraordinary floods, storms, lightning, etc.

Other Acts

A carrier is not liable for other acts, such as acts of public enemy, acts of public authority, and acts or omissions of the shipper, or for the inherent nature of or vice in the goods.

Carriers must make every reasonable effort to minimize any loss due to an Act of God or of the other acts mentioned above, and they would be held responsible if they did not take reasonable steps to prevent unnecessary additional damage.

Specifying Date of Delivery

Shippers cannot mark the bill of lading with a definite delivery date.

The carrier's duty is to move the goods within a reasonable period; he may not contract to transport and deliver other than with reasonable dispatch.

Labor Disturbances

The bill of lading provides that a carrier will not be liable for loss or damage due to delay of a shipment because of riots or strikes.

Delay in Shipment

If the carrier has knowledge of an undue and unreasonable delay in delivery, he should notify the shipper and consignee.

Acceptance of Late Shipment

The consignee is required to accept late shipments caused by an unreasonable delay unless the consignee can show that the goods are thereby rendered worthless.

The carrier is liable for payment of damages resulting from unreasonable delay, the liability being the difference between the current value of the goods and their value if they had been delivered within a reasonable period.

Seasonal Goods

Courts have generally held that unreasonable delay on seasonal types of goods does not give the consignee the right to refuse the goods.

Either the consignee or the shipper should accept the goods and file claim for damages resulting from such delay, the amount being the difference between the value of the goods on the date delivered and their value if they had been delivered with reasonable dispatch.

The word "seasonal" has a broad meaning, especially with regard to fabrics and garments, as there always appears to be a market for both, be it discounters, basement and budget operations, jobbers, or exporters.

Seasonal claims that result in litigation may lead to delays and legal expenses unwarranted by the amount involved. It may be advisable to seek compensation for the difference in market values (wholesale difference, not retail difference, is normally the limit of recovery).

Refusals by Consignee

The consignee may not refuse the goods because they have been damaged in the course of shipment, unless the damage results in an almost total loss.

Under normal conditions, the consignee must accept the goods and hold the carrier responsible for the damage done.

Refusal of Part of a Shipment

Unless the goods have become of trifling value or totally unsalable because of delay, the consignee must accept such goods and hold the carrier responsible for the loss caused by the delay.

Refused Goods Returned to Shipper

The same rule applies as to the original shipment; the carrier, upon receipt of return instructions, is required to return the goods within a reasonable period. This return movement constitutes a new shipment, and the carrier may require a new bill of lading to be executed by the consignee of the original shipment.

If the goods are returned unreasonably late to the original shipper, the consignee (in this case the original shipper) is still obligated to accept the shipment, as he now becomes the "owner," having instructed the carrier to return the shipment. As owner, the consignee is now required to file a claim against the carrier for the difference in the market value.

Notice of Refusal

If the shipments are refused by the consignee, or if the consignee cannot be located, the carrier is obligated to take the following steps before he can legally dispose of the refused goods:

He must, after such refusal or failure to locate consignee, promptly mail to both the shipper and the consignee a notice of refused or on-hand freight.

This notice gives the details of the shipment and the consignee's name, pro number, on-hand address, and reasons for refusal or nondelivery. The notice also advises the consignee and the shipper that if disposition is not directed within fifteen days after its receipt, the goods will be disposed of in accordance with the provisions of the Uniform Carrier Bill of Lading.

Salvage

The sections of the Uniform Carrier Bill of Lading applicable to salvage read as follows:

> (4b) Where nonperishable property has been transported to destination hereunder is refused by consignee or the party entitled to receive it upon tender of delivery, or said consignee or party entitled to receive it fails to receive or claim it within 15 days after notice of arrival shall have been duly sent or given, the carrier may sell same at public auction to the highest bidder, at such place as may be designated by the carrier:
>
> PROVIDED, That the carrier shall have at first mailed, sent, or given to the consignee notice that the property has been refused or remains unclaimed, as the case may be, and that it will be subject to sale under the terms of the bill of lading if disposition is not arranged for, and shall have published notice containing a description of the property, the name of the party to whom consigned, or if shipped order notify, the name of the party to be notified and the time and place of sale, once a week for two consecutive weeks, in a newspaper of general circulation at the place of sale or nearest place, where such newspaper is published. Provided, that 30 days shall have elapsed before publication of notice of sale after said notice that the property was refused or remains unclaimed was mailed, sent or given.
>
> (4c) perishable property
>
> (4d) Where the procedure provided for in the two paragraphs last preceding is not possible, it is agreed that nothing in said paragraphs shall be construed to abridge the right of the carrier, at its option, to sell the property under such circumstances and in such manner as may be authorized by law.
>
> (4e) The proceeds of any sale made under this section shall be applied by the carrier to the payment of freight, demurrage, storage, and any other lawful charges and the expense of notice, advertisement, sale, and other necessary expense and of caring for and maintaining the property, if proper care of same requires special expense, and should there be a balance it shall be paid to the owner of the property sold hereunder.

Insurance

While it is generally true that carriers are liable for loss or damage owing to their own negligence, most shippers carry "inland marine insurance" to protect themselves in case the carrier is unable to make a satisfactory voluntary settlement of claims or lacks sufficient means to pay, or in the event of an Act of God or other acts for which the carrier may not be responsible.

The claimant would not be able to collect from both the carrier and the insurance company, as the insurance company would require the claimant to subrogate its claim against the carrier to the insurance company.

Returns from Outside the U.S.

It is best to endeavor to arrange an allowance so as to dissuade any consignee from returning any goods from an area outside the continental United States.

Considering the amount of inward and outward transportation charges, insurance, duties, and delays that are involved, especially for seasonal goods, such returns should be avoided by arranging a reasonable allowance.

If this cannot be done, and if the salesman resides in the area, it is best to have him take possession of the goods and endeavor to arrange a resale in the same area.

chapter eighteen

TRACING AND EXPEDITING SHIPMENTS

Nonarrival Notice to Shipper

A consignee will call and advise that an expected shipment has not arrived. In many instances the merchandise is required for a planned advertisement, and the buyer is frantic that the goods will arrive after the advertisement has run or that the merchandise manager will require the buyer to pull the ad.

Expediting Shipments

If a consignee requires an undelayed shipment, the carrier's representative is informed as soon as practicable and requested to alert all concerned as to the necessity of a prompt and undelayed shipment. (See Letter A on page 119.)

Information Required for a Tracer

Name of shipper
Point of shipment
Date on signed bill of lading
Number of cartons
Weight of shipment
Name of consignee
Address of consignee
Full routing
Pro number
Trailer number (if known)

Notification to Carrier

The tracer is best handled by the distribution plant, as all the information required is available to the plant.

Names and Telephone Numbers of Carriers

The distribution plant should have a list of the major carriers throughout the United States. This list, including name, address, telephone number, and manager's name, is available at nominal cost from various carriers' associations.

Follow-up

Information should be telephoned in to the originating carrier and confirmed in writing. The name of the person spoken to should be requested, and this person should be asked to return the call and provide pertinent information such as the date of delivery to the connecting carrier and the connecting carrier's name, address, and telephone number. (See Letter B on page 119.)

The shipper should contact the connecting carrier and request a return call advising of the date of expected delivery and the reason for the delay.

Advice to Consignee

The consignee should be given copies of all letters to the originating and connecting carriers. The consignee, with the above information, is in an excellent position to contact the delivering carrier for information as to final delivery.

The consignee should notify the shipper as soon as the shipment is received so that the tracer can be withdrawn.

Delays

Many delays occur because the originating carrier turns over the goods to a connecting carrier that is not licensed to service the area of the consignee.

The connecting carrier may then have to return the goods to the originating carrier, which then has to transfer the goods to another connecting carrier able to service the area.

Mismarking

Many delays are caused because the shipper lists an incorrect address or abbreviation of city and state—for example, Springfield, Ohio, instead of Springfield, Massachusetts.

Tracing

When connecting carriers are employed, tracing is more involved and often frustrating.

Some carriers handle tracers efficiently, whereas others, such as express companies and air-connecting carriers, are more difficult to deal with.

Daily telephone calls are almost a necessity in order to obtain a quicker delivery and to determine the source of the difficulty causing the delay. Local representatives of delivering carriers are helpful in tracing and expediting shipments and one should become acquainted with them.

Replacement

When information as to the final date of delivery is difficult to obtain, or if the goods appear to be lost, a quick replacement may be necessary to satisfy the customer's needs. (See Letter B on page 118.)

chapter nineteen

FILING OF A CLAIM

Time Limit

Claims must be filed in writing within nine months after delivery.

In case of failure to make a delivery, the claim must be filed in writing within nine months after a reasonable time for delivery has elapsed.

Amending a Claim

The claimant can amend the claim at any time until the claim is actually paid.

Intention to File a Claim

Intention to file a claim should not be considered due notice of filing a claim and should also not be considered as having filed a claim within the time limit.

Legal Suit

Institution of filing a legal suit is set at two years and a day from the day when notice in writing is given by the carrier to the claimant that the carrier has disallowed the claim or any part thereof specified in the notice of filing a claim.

Registered Mail, Return Receipt

Claims should be sent by registered mail, return receipt requested, so as to avoid a carrier's contention that a claim in writing was not received.

Filing a Claim against the Originating or Delivering Carrier

Either the originating carrier or the delivering carrier is bound by law to pay any legitimate claim filed with it by the claimant, regardless of whether or not the particular carrier was at fault.

Usually the owner, or consignee, should file the claim against the delivering carrier, for the owner has a better relationship with that carrier and is more apt to obtain a satisfactory and prompt settlement.

There are times when it is advisable because of the nature of the resource-customer relationship for the shipper to file the claim. Again, the resource should file against the originating carrier, as the resource usually gives the carrier a sizable volume of business, knows the carrier's representatives, and is in a position to obtain a prompt and fair settlement.

Requirement of Written Claim

While most carriers issue their own claim form, there are five basic requirements for filing a claim:

1. Notice that the loss has occurred.
2. Notice of the nature of the loss
3. Notice of the nature of the shipment involved

4. Information of the date of shipment, point of origin, and point of destination

5. Notice that the parties to the shipment expect restitution and reimbursement, and the amount so requested

The necessary supporting papers, sufficient to permit investigation of the claim, must be filed before the carrier can make a settlement.

Minimum Filing Requirements

Original bill of lading

Paid freight bill

Original or certified copy of invoice

Copy of carrier's receipt, listing exceptions (shortages, damages, wet cartons, etc.)

Copy of inspection report (carrier's or consignee's invoice for loss sustained) listing actual dollars being claimed and the reasons for the claim (loss, damage, injury, delay, etc.)

Shipper's certification

Documents Not Constituting a Claim

Bad-order reports

Appraisal reports of damage

Claims filed for uncertain amounts

Notations of shortage or damage (or both) on freight bills, delivery receipts, or other documents, or inspection reports issued by the carriers or their inspection agencies—whether the extent of the loss or damage is indicated in dollars and cents or otherwise—shall, standing alone, not be considered by the carriers as sufficient to comply with the minimum claim-filing requirements specified by the ICC regulations.

Acknowledgment of Claims

The carrier shall, upon receipt of a written claim, give it a claim number and refer to the claim and the claim number in an acknowledgment of the claim, which must be sent within thirty days after the receipt of the claim.

Additional Documents Required by the Carrier

The carrier is required, when acknowledging the claim, to request any additional documentary evidence or other pertinent information required in order to process the claim, as a preliminary examination of the claim, as filed, may have revealed that more information was required.

Investigation of Loss

Each claim filed against a carrier shall, in accordance with ICC regulations, be promptly investigated.

Disposition of Claim

The carrier is obligated to pay, decline, or make a firm compromise offer in writing to the claimant within 120 days after receipt of the claim. If, however, the claim cannot be processed and disposed of within 120 days after the receipt thereof, the carrier shall at that time, and at the expiration of each succeeding sixty-day period while the claim remains pending, advise the claimant in writing of the status of the claim and the reason for the delay in making final disposition of it.

Late Receipt of Missing Package

A prerequisite of the voluntary payment by a carrier of a claim for loss (shortage) of an entire package or an entire shipment shall be the securing by the carrier of a certified statement in writing, from the consignee of the shipment involved, that the property for which the claim is filed has not been received from any source.

Claim Exclusions

Claims to be settled on a voluntary basis by the carrier may not include the following:

Attorneys' fees
Interest charges
Clerical fees
Consequential damage

Proposed Legislation Recommended by the ICC

The ICC has proposed the following legislation to be enacted by the Congress of the United States:

> Adjudication of Claims by the Interstate Commerce Commission
>
> Notwithstanding any other provisions of the Interstate Commerce Act, all actions brought under and by virtue of paragraph 20 (11) of that act against a carrier (except those that may include claims for the recovery of attorneys' fees) shall be brought in the first instance only before the Interstate Commerce Commission by the filing of a complaint in writing setting forth therein the nature of the action and the amount of the money claimed therefor, and the order of the Interstate Commerce Commission shall be binding upon all parties to such disputes unless otherwise revised on judicial review: Provided, That issues arising in the determination of such actions shall be determined in the most expeditious manner and, so far as practical and legally permissible, without formal hearings or other proceedings; And Provided further, That in all actions filed with the Interstate Commerce Commission in accordance with this paragraph, appellate review of the orders of the Commission issued to dispose of such matters shall only be by a district court of the United States in a district through or into which the defendant carrier operates, and any aggrieved party shall, upon request timely made to the court, receive an opportunity for a trial before a jury as to disputed issues of fact.
>
> (At the time of publication of this book, Congress had not acted on this proposed legislation.)

Insurance

It must be remembered that while common carriers are held responsible for the full amount of any loss or damage for which they are responsible, there are other types of carriers that limit their liability for any one shipment.

It is therefore incumbent upon the shipper and the consignee to acquaint themselves with the limited amount of insurance of the carriers they use or designate, especially local and noninterstate carriers.

Some of the amounts are as follows:

Deliverers to airlines	$ 50
Express companies	50
Airlines	50
Local carriers	50
Parcel forwarders	100

The rates for the above carriers include the coverage on claims for the above amounts. Additional coverage is available by paying an additional modest charge.

In the absence of specific instructions to the contrary, shippers should include full coverage when making shipments, on the theory that the consignees may hold them liable if they do not provide the coverage; in addition, the consignee pays for the transportation charge which would include such coverage.

Parcel Post Shipments

Parcel post shipments do not include insurance coverage, unless so designated and paid for. As the consignee is charged for the postage, it again is to the advantage of the shipper to cover the value of the goods being shipped.

Many consignees have parcel post shipments included in their inland marine insurance policy.

When the consignee designates "no insurance," the shipper should only obtain a 5-cent receipt so that he can prove that the shipment has been made.

Some consignees are under the impression that claims for concealed loss or concealed damages on parcel post shipments are unrecoverable.

There is a space on the claim form for the inclusion of such claims, and if the amount is not too great and no inspection is required, then the claim is usually honored.

Self-Insurance

Some shippers charge the customers for the full amount of the insurance, although they do not obtain the insurance for the shipment. They do obtain a 5-cent receipt to prove delivery.

By self-insuring, they figure that over a year's time they will show a profit after paying consignees' claims for any undelivered shipments.

chapter twenty

SAMPLE LETTERS AND FORMS

RETURNS AND REFUSALS

Letter A on page 67

Dear ________

We are in receipt of advice from ________
(carrier)
that you have refused a shipment made by us to you on ______.
(date)

We do not know the reason for this refusal or whether or not your refusal is justifiable due to our failure to comply with the terms of your order.

If, however, this refusal was caused for any reason beyond our control, then we wish to disclaim any responsibility for any loss incurred due to such refusal.

The general rule is that title to merchandise shipped passes to the consignee upon delivery of such merchandise to the carrier for transportation to the destination.

It is also the rule that the owner is the proper person to file a claim against the carrier for any loss or damage that is sustained in transit.

The consignee is obligated to accept late shipments caused by unreasonable delay by the carrier, unless he can show that the goods to be rendered are worthless.

Under an ordinary bill of lading, the consignee may not as a general rule reject the goods and then hold the carrier liable for any injury that is the fault of the consignee.

The carrier holding refused shipments may, after certain notices and periods of time, sell the refused goods in order to recoup storage and forwarding charges. As expressed above, we will not be responsible for any losses incurred due to such sale by the carrier unless it can be proved that we violated the terms of the order.

Yours truly,

(Registered mail, return receipt requested)

Letter B on page 67

To the Controller:

In view of the notices of sales sent to us by the carrier (as per enclosed copies), we are writing to you to enlist your good services in our desire to amicably resolve the matter covered by the enclosed copies of letters.

Your cooperation in this regard will be greatly appreciated.

Yours truly,

Letter A on page 68

Dear __________ :

We are in receipt of a return forwarded by you to our office __________ *(show room)* in __________ *(city)*.

Our invoices and return stickers call your attention to the fact that all authorized returns are to be sent to our distribution plant in __________ *(city)*.

We do not have the space or facilities to handle such returns in __________ *(city)*. In addition, we are forced to expend additional effort and pay additional charges for this return to our distribution plant.

In the future we shall refuse such returns and ask your cooperation in directing such returns to the distribution plant in __________ *(city, state)*.

Yours truly,

TRACING AND EXPEDITING SHIPMENTS

Letter B on page 108

Dear __________ :

This will confirm our telephone conversation today in which we advised that the carrier __________ to date has not been able to locate the goods covered by our invoice number _____ dated _____.

Please advise us if you desire that we make a replacement shipment, and specify the routing you want us to use in order to expedite the delivery to you.

Yours truly,

Letter A on page 105

To the Carrier:

This will confirm our telephone conversation with you on this date, in which we requested that you make every effort to expedite the delivery to the consignee:

Name
Address
City State Zip

This shipment, consisting of ____ cartons weighing _____ , was signed for by your driver as __________

Your efforts in this regard will be appreciated. Please advise when the consignee may expect shipment.

Yours truly,

Letter B on page 106

To the Carrier:

This will confirm our telephone conversation today in which we requested that you trace and prove delivery of the shipment to:

Name
Address
City State Zip

via __________ number of cartons ____ weight
pro number____ trailer

Please phone the writer as to the progress in locating this shipment, and advise as to when the shipment will be delivered so that we can notify the consignee.

Yours truly,

(copy to connecting carrier)
(copy to consignee . . . Please advise when

delivery is made so that we can withdraw both the tracer and the request for proof of delivery.)

Yours truly,

CONCEALED LOSS AND DAMAGE

Letter on page 42

Dear ________:

We are in receipt of your form reply regarding the above claim. Evidently you are not familiar with the provisions covering a concealed loss (shortage) claim.

The carrier who delivered the goods to you issues regulations requiring that in the event of a concealed loss claim you notify the carrier by phone, confirmed in writing, within forty-eight hours to fifteen days, depending on the particular carrier, after receipt of the merchandise and that you hold intact the cartons and merchandise for a joint inspection.

The carrier is then required to make a reasonably fast joint inspection; if this inspection is not made by the carrier, you are permitted to make your own inspection, filling out an Inspection Report of Loss or Damage Discovered after Delivery (such forms are provided by your carrier).

If you have requested an inspection, please send us a copy of the report; if you have not, you are barred from making a claim for concealed loss or damage against the carrier in the expectation that the carrier may legally make a voluntary settlement of the claim if satisfied that neither you nor the shipper contributed toward the loss.

Our plant has verified that the weights are correct for the amounts shipped against the invoices for which you are making a claim for loss (shortage).

Because we feel that you evidently were not acquainted with the regulations covering concealed loss or damage claims, we are willing to issue credit for one-half the amount requested by you, but in the future you will have to abide by the carriers' regulations regarding concealed loss (shortage) or damage claims.

Please advise us concerning the above.

Yours truly,

RETURNS DUE TO SHOW-ROOM ERRORS

Letter A on page 90

Dear __________:

We are in receipt of your notice requesting that we cancel the order for styles __________ (or balance).

We wish to advise that a shipment covering the styles (or balance) was made prior to receipt of your notice.

Since this shipment was made in good faith and within the shipping period designated on the order, we request that you accept it, as we feel confident that it will prove valuable for timely (or seasonal) selling.

Yours truly,

RETURNS DUE TO CUSTOMER PROBLEMS

Letter B on page 93

Dear __________:

We are in receipt of your letter dated _____ requesting a return sticker for styles _____ that you claimed were not ordered by you.

We are enclosing herewith a copy of your order, listing the above styles.

Since this shipment was made in good faith, we request that you offer the goods for sale, as we are confident that they will prove valuable for timely (or seasonal) selling.

Yours truly,

RETURNS DUE TO FABRIC DAMAGES

Letter B on pages 71 and 73

Dear ________ :

We hereby notify you of a latent defect with regard to your fabric ________, pattern
(name)
number _____, color _____, covered by your invoice number _____ dated _____ and in the amount of _____ .

We request that you arrange to have your quality control man contact us with regard to the above.

Yours truly,

Registered mail-return receipt

RETURNS DUE TO MANUFACTURING DAMAGES AND PACKAGING ERRORS

Letter C on pages 81 and 97

Dear ________ :

We acknowledge receipt of your letter dated _______ advising of a missing ________.
(name of part)

We are forwarding same to you via air mail special delivery.

We regret very much any inconvenience caused you, and we appreciate your cooperation.

Thank you.

Yours truly,

RETURN STICKER

From	No. Authorized return ______
______	Amount authorized ______
Address ______	Debit memo ______
City ______	Routing ______
State ______	Insure ______
Zip # ______	No. insurance ______

SHIP TO ______

STREET ADDRESS ______

CITY ______ STATE ______ ZIP # ______

Routing ______

Contents: Merchandise - Fourth Class Mail
Postmaster: This parcel may be opened for inspection
if necessary
RETURN POSTAGE GUARANTEED

(See paragraph titled Return Sticker on page 64.)

POSTCARD CHANGE IN ORDER

Please note corrections on Date ____________ 197__

Order # ____________ Dept. ____________

Style # Listed Should be

Price ____________

Price ____________

Price ____________

Delivery ____________

Delivery ____________

Delivery ____________

Terms ____________

From ____________

Address ____________ City ____________ State ____________ Zip # ____

Phone # ____________

(See paragraphs titled Price-Change Card on page 16 and Delivery Schedule on page 88.)

CREDIT INDEX CARD

Face

NAME____________________ account # __________

St. address ______________ county________ rating________

City____________ State____ zip # ________ cred. code ________

Collect suit________ insuf funds____________ chap 11 ________

Cod________ cbd ______ post dated____________ state-date________

remarks________________________ declined________

Short date	claims $	remarks	unjust date	returns $	remarks

Owner's name tel #

Control name

Reverse Side

ORDERS

date	div.	$	date	div.	$	date	div.	$	date	div.	$

(See paragraphs titled Customer's Claim and Credit Index Card on page 3; Index Cards on page 61; and Quality Not Good Enough on page 93.)

INDEX CARD AT DISTRIBUTION PLANT

Name ____________________ acct. # __________

St. address ____________________ county __________

City _______________ State __________ zip # __________

Invoices _______________ copies to __________

Duplicates _______________ on carton __________

Cancellations: do not ship after (date) _______________

Substitutions allowed __________ not allowed __________

Back orders allowed __________ not allowed __________ prepay __________

Size change allowed __________ not allowed __________

Routing _______________ insure __________

1 ____ lb. to ____ lbs. __________ insure __________

____ lb. to ____ lbs. __________ insure __________

Over ________ lbs. __________ insure __________

PP ________ UPS ________ EXP ________ AIR ________ Insure ________

Penalty ____________________

____

Other ____________________

(See paragraphs titled Customer's Index Card in the Distribution Plant and Copy of Index Card Attached to Order on page 6; Customer's Index Card on page 8; and Automatic Cancellation on page 84.)

INDEX